Lamentations
and the
Tears of the World

Lamentations
and the
Tears of the World

Kathleen M. O'Connor

ORBIS BOOKS

Maryknoll, New York 10545

Founded in 1970, Orbis Books endeavors to publish works that enlighten the mind, nourish the spirit, and challenge the conscience. The publishing arm of the Maryknoll Fathers & Brothers, Orbis seeks to explore the global dimensions of the Christian faith and mission, to invite dialogue with diverse cultures and religious traditions, and to serve the cause of reconciliation and peace. The books published reflect the views of their authors and do not represent the official position of the Maryknoll Society. To learn more about Maryknoll and Orbis Books, please visit our website at www.maryknoll.com.

Queries regarding rights and permissions should be addressed to: Orbis Books, P.O. Box 308, Maryknoll, New York 10545-0308.

Published by Orbis Books, Maryknoll, NY 10545-0308
Manuscript editing and typesetting by Joan Weber Laflamme
Manufactured in the United States of America

Library of Congress Cataloging-in-Publication Data

O'Connor, Kathleen M., 1942-
    Lamentations and the tears of the world / Kathleen M. O'Connor.
      p. cm.
    Includes bibliographical references (p.)
    ISBN 1-57075-399-7
    1. Bible. O.T. Lamentations—Criticism, interpretation, etc. I. Title.

BS1535.52.O25 2002
224'3077—dc21

                           2001051340

For Jim

Contents

Part I
Commentary: Who Will Comfort You?

Part II
Reflections: A Theology of Witness

Foreword

WALTER BRUEGGEMANN

Since her original research on the "Confession of Jeremiah," Kathleen O'Connor, my distinguished and treasured colleague, has been pondering the Old Testament texts that voice Israel's grief to God in the passionate expectation that Israel's insistence, in sadness and candor, will evoke from God gifts of newness. She has understood well, for a long time, the extraordinary power of these texts, both their artistic sensibility and the daring measure of faith that is brought to voice.

In the present book, however, O'Connor has taken a giant leap forward, both in her own daring presentation and in the way she carries readers to new depths of human anguish and human hope as she lets these texts have their full say. O'Connor offers a full, careful, and elegant commentary of the Book of Lamentations, in which she detects the troubled, unsettled range of voices that speak; only on the completion of the "commentary" does she launch into her rich and shamelessly beautiful theological exposition. Her way with a phrase, her sense of woundedness-cum-denial, her stark theological judgment all converge to make a mesmerizing statement. The word that comes to mind for the book is *exquisite* . . . in every way. Who else, in eight pages, could line out in sequence such phrases as:

- Prayer as Truthfulness
- Lamentations as Impassioned Hope
- Lamentations as a Work of Justice
- The Power of Tears
- Weeping as a Political Act
- Prayers of Lament Teach Resistance
- Justice and Solidarity

It is all there, leaving us breathless, wanting more, but fully satisfied because truth in its deep, rich capacity is before us.

This book will stand on its own as a breakthrough that invites believers in many traditions and scholars in many disciplines to pay fresh attention. In light of the events of September 11, of course, O'Connor's book may be "the scroll" that will mediate life . . . fully fractured, utterly hope-filled, deeply comforted. The book is "for Jim," but the rest of us will stand close in sharing it.

Preface

I began working on Lamentations for another project the year my husband, Jim Griesmer, was receiving extensive infusions in the oncology room at Columbia Presbyterian Medical Center in New York City. He has a neuropathy, not cancer, but at the time the outcome of his treatments seemed as uncertain as if it were cancer. As I worked on the biblical text in the infusion room for hours and months at a time, waiting for his long treatments to end, the worlds of the text, of the cancer center, and of my own inner being crossed over and replicated parts of one another in startling loops of communication.

In the infusion center, a United Nations of the ill surrounded us. Old and young people from many ethnic and racial backgrounds were fighting for their lives. Grief and fear, resignation and hope resided in the room together, overlapping, interlacing, and struggling with each other. On various days, among various patients, one emotion might prevail over the other but not for long. Soon the uneasy alliances between hope and dread, anger and impatience reasserted themselves, as if the room required these pendulum swings to remain upright.

In the midst of this intense, struggling life presided nurses and staff, efficient, tender, and wise beyond their collective years, as though somehow their encounters with the courageous and despairing had made of them altered beings, more compassionate and gentle, more fully human than most. They ministered to their patients with knowing acceptance. They saw and received pain and slowly helped patients put words to it. They accepted fear and rage, along with the physical and spiritual manifestations of disease. They spoke with their patients as human beings, learned about their families, their lives, and treated them as agents in their own care. Together they enacted the theological insight at the core of this book that I call "a theology of witnessing."

I find the bare bones of such a theology in Lamentations, a biblical book of five poems, all expressing pain, fury, and despair in an intense struggle for life. The many speaking voices in the poetry beg God to be their witness, to see them, pay attention to them, and receive them in their pain. God never responds in Lamentations, but the book itself becomes a comforting witness. It is a "house for sorrow" (Mintz 2) and a safe place for tears. It honors voices of loss, pain, and despair. It mirrors pain back to those who suffer and, in the process, brings them out of isolation into community, even if only briefly. It has done so for me, not only in coming to terms with Jim's life-altering medical condition, but in my lifelong search for wholeness.

Lamentations is about the collapse of a physical, emotional, and spiritual universe of an entire people, not about individual sorrows except in a metaphoric and symbolic manner. Yet the power of its poetry can embrace the sufferings of any whose bodies and spirits are worn down and assaulted, whose boundaries have shrunk, who are trapped, and who face foreclosed futures. And although, or perhaps because, Lamentations holds intense personal resonance for me, I find in it ethical challenges to my American society, as well as a tool for cultural and social healing.

I refer often to Canadian theologian Douglas John Hall's perceptive social analysis of North American culture, by which he means the wealthy societies of the United States and Canada, not Mexico. He proposes that we live under a deadening blanket of "covert despair," a despair fostered by wealth, power, and violence that distract us from our spiritual hunger, alienation, and meaninglessness. The argument of my book is that Lamentations can be a resource for the work of reclaiming our humanity, for breaking through our denial, personal and social, and for teaching us compassion. Lamentations urges us to do the difficult work of reclaiming our passion for life, for justice and empathy. Without such work we will never be able to hear the cries of the poor in our neighborhood or around the globe. Our own wounds, hidden and festering, will continue to enslave us, absorbing all our energies in fruitless denial that blocks our ears and blinds our eyes.

Lamentations hardly needs interpretation for peoples who live in the ruins of destroyed cities, whose societies are decimated by genocide, or who barely subsist in the face of famine and poverty. When I wrote this book, I had no way of knowing I would live among them. The events of September 11, 2001, and their aftermath, have brought images from lamentations alive before our eyes.

In Part I, "Who Will Comfort You?," I present a commentary on each of the book's five poems, preceded by an introductory chapter on poetic beauty and interpretive puzzles of Lamentations. In my commentary I focus on the speaking voices or "characters" in the text as they struggle to articulate their pain and to cope with the aftermath of trauma. The voices offer conflicting testimonies about their experiences of suffering and about God, and Lamentations makes no effort to resolve the conflicts. Instead, it juxtaposes hope and despair. The voices malign and assault God, but God never replies.

By leaving out the voice of God, the book gives undistracted reverence to human voices of pain and resistance. Yet the book is profoundly theological, for it challenges all theologies of a God who dotes on our personal and national wishes.

In Part II, I reflect on Lamentations for my context. I believe it is immoral to interpret texts for lives of people other than one's own, but I hope that my comments might spawn different interpretations for other contexts. My reflective efforts begin from an ongoing "hermeneutics of suspicion," a doubting and questioning distrust of the text and, most particularly, of this culture, but they attempt to serve more directly what Dorothee Soelle (45-49) calls "a hermeneutics of hunger." When I interpret Lamentations, I am doing more than critiquing ideologies of text and society. With Soelle (48), I seek connections between the hunger of the world's poor and the hunger of the First World, a hunger that is no "less life threatening."

I am convinced that our profound spiritual hunger undermines not only our own humanity; it also affects our relationships with other peoples and with the earth itself. We feed that hunger in our frenzied self-centeredness and with anesthetizing abundance and violence. This is the "spiritual catastrophe in which the rich live" (Soelle 48), and it continues to endanger the world. I find in Lamentations food for this hunger and a healing balm for hidden wounds. The hunger of the rich is not comparable to the material hungers of the poor, but our inhumanity, our inability to be empathic, and our denial of our own deep hungers directly impinge upon the lives of the poor, who often have much to teach us about humanity.

Many conversations, biblical, theological, and personal, have fed this book like hidden, barely traceable nourishing streams. I rejoice in them all.

Doctor of Ministry students in classes at Columbia Theological Seminary, participants in workshops at Columbia Theological Seminary, at the Maryknoll Sisters Center, at Misericordia Bible Institute, at the Marianella Retreat House in Dublin, Ireland, walked through Lamentations with me and told how the book challenged them, comforted them, and illumined their ministries.

Professors Chip Dobbs-Allsopp, Tod Linafelt, and Nancy Lee—all creative scholars of Lamentations—generously shared their work with me.

Orbis Editor Sue Perry took encouraging interest in my fascination with Lamentations and has been exceedingly patient.

Student assistants Jonathan Kaplan and Rick Olson did library searches and copyediting. Ms. Tempie Alexander has been a most precise technical assistant and kind friend.

Sr. Grace Meyerjack, M.M., Dr. Sarah Lopez, Lilli Baxter, Charlotte Keller, Lalor Ferrari, and Rev. Julie Johnson engaged my questions and urged me on.

Columbia Theological Seminary colleagues Professors George Stroup and Margit Ernst have argued with me about God and texts.

Professors Walter Brueggemann and Christine Yoder have listened to my laments, laughed with me in our common work, and with questions, resources, and readings encouraged me at every turn. In colleagueship, they are unsurpassed.

Jim has been my witness.

Part I

Commentary

Who Will Comfort You?

1

Poetry of Loss: A Defense

Lamentations presents the pain of survivors in the aftermath of the destruction of Jerusalem. The city's collapse after a military invasion left a wide swath of destruction in the life of the people. They lost loved ones, a way of life, and material well-being; they lost hope for the future and confidence in God. Lamentations is a short book of five poems that expresses with searing clarity their fear, grief, and despair. The book is an artistic jewel, a theological enigma, and a courageous act of survival. Because it contains rich, metaphoric poetry, it is able to embrace the sorrows of the world.

When people learn I am studying Lamentations, they often wonder if I do not find the book "depressing." I answer with an emphatic "No!" To me, Lamentations is not depressing; it cannot cause sorrow, hostility, or despair; it cannot evoke emotions readers do not already know. Rather than creating pain, it reveals pain. It is a disturbing book, nonetheless, because it can lure into the open experiences, memories, and feelings many people prefer to deny. It can draw poison from wounds and expose realities entire societies and individuals dismiss from consciousness because seeing them might undermine their worlds.

A Book of Comfort

For readers who begin from a place of suffering, Lamentations is a book of comfort. It serves as a witness, a knowing, a form of seeing, wherein readers recognize their lives, symbolically or more literally, and in that recognition they are no longer alone in their pain. We enter a poetic space that, no matter how distant from our own lives, has strange capacities for assurance and companionship. Within its poetry, we can say, "Yes, that resembles my life," now or in the past or perhaps in the future. Curiously, perhaps paradoxically, by focusing on suffering, by bringing it into the open, and reflecting it back to readers, Lamentations offers solace. Nearly bereft of comfort itself, the book is immensely comforting.

But for readers who live with denial, as the United States' capitalist society requires, Lamentations makes difficult reading, indeed. Douglas Hall (130) asserts that "covert despair—repressed hopelessness" characterizes the spiritual condition of North American culture. Unlike the despair of the poor and afflicted around the globe who know too well their true condition, the despair of the dominant culture of North America is a denied despair, not merely hidden by wealth and power but forcibly refused. This is, of course, a survival tactic since humans "know at a deeper level than conscious thought, that survival depends upon hope" (Hall 131). Despair, therefore, is not even allowed to the level of consciousness.

But denial as a mode of survival differs from "the kind of repressive posture that must lie to itself consistently that it ends in destructive behavior more devastating than the negating realities it fears to acknowledge" (Hall 131). To bring our despair into consciousness would reveal our exhausted spirits, our broken communities, and our violent relationships at home and abroad. The question for Hall is whether Christianity has "enough imagination and daring" to help us find a way into the future (Hall 142). Lamentations may provide one such tool.

Lamentations' testimony is bitter, raw, and largely unhealed. Its poems use "wounded words" (Forché 41-46) to illumine pain and resist God's acts in the world. In its ragged struggles to articulate suffering and arrive at hope, it peers into wounds and raises fierce questions about God. Aggressively confronting suffering and resolutely refusing to whitewash truth, Lamentations has become for me a mirror of my wounds and of the wounds of the world. For all its brutality, I find in it an invitation to life. This book is an unapologetic defense of Lamentations. It lauds its capacity to overcome denial, personal and political, to lead toward healing and compassion, and to release life's energies for the work of justice and praise.

A Work of Art

Lamentations is a potent work of art. To read it is to enter into a world apart, a world created by suggestion, image, and metaphor. Because it is an imagined symbolic world, it can, like all good poetry, intermingle with our real worlds to reveal, mirror, and challenge them. In this conversation between worlds, it can help us see our pain, and, by reflecting it back to us, however indirectly, it has the potential to affirm our human dignity in a first step toward healing. Such is the power of art.

Mintz (3) aptly calls Lamentations a "shelter for sorrow," but it evokes readers' worlds in different ways. For survivors of civil wars, destroyed cities, and genocides, for refugees, and for those who subsist in famine and destitute poverty, the poetry mirrors reality with frightening exactitude. When, like me, readers live in relative safety and prosperity, Lamentations calls forth loss and pain more narrowly, personally, and indirectly. Yet even in the prosperous United States there are normal human losses to lament, deaths, disappointments, and hidden depression with which to contend. There are broken marriages, catastrophic illnesses, and violence among our children, hatred between groups, and debilitating poverty exacerbated by wealth all around. Behind the wealth and power of the United States hide despair and a violent culture of denial that drains our humanity. For our sake and for the sake of the world over which we try callously to preside, these things demand lamentation.

Whether extreme suffering can or should be rendered into art has been a pressing question after the Nazi Holocaust of the Jews in the middle of the last century. Many Holocaust survivors insist that art trivializes "radical suffering," a term of Wendy Farley's that refers to suffering "when the negativity of a situation is experienced as an assault upon one's personhood *as such*" (Farley 53). It degrades that which makes the person most human. Art about such suffering is impossible, the argument goes, because it can never be commensurate with the experience.

Aaron Zeitlin writes about the problem of finding words both to encompass and to reveal the unspeakable suffering wrought by the Holocaust. "Were Jeremiah to sit by the ashes of Israel today, he would not cry out an 'ēkāh, a Lamentation . . . the Almighty himself would be powerless to open his well of tears" (Niger 14). The act of lamenting is impossible, claims Zeitlin, because the impact of the Holocaust is beyond compare in its evil destructiveness. But such suffering is also more literally unspeakable because profound pain destroys victims' capacity for speech. It renders victims numb, wordless, and further isolates them in their pain. In Zeitlin's view, the massive suffering of the Holocaust would silence even the prophet and block the tears of God were they to consider responding to it.

Yet decades later Holocaust survivors have produced an ever-burgeoning library of testimony. They have been able to bring into speech "some equivalent of the world within a world" of their experience (Teichman and Leder 6) in what we might call "a poetry of truth-telling." Truth-telling is an act of survival, because it affirms the humanity of victims, gives them agency, and places a wedge between their experience of suffering and its expression. Lamentations is ancient poetry of truth-telling, an act of survival that testifies to the human requirement to speak the unspeakable, to find speech in traumatized numbness, and, to borrow a phrase from Linafelt, to assert boldly the "sheer fact of pain."

The poetry of Lamentations arose in the aftermath of a catastrophic historical event, the destruction of Jerusalem, but what is not certain is after which of the many invasions of the city. Ancient tradition places the book in the sixth century B.C.E., following three military assaults upon the city by the Babylonians (597, 587, and 582 B.C.E.). The Septuagint or Greek translation of Lamentations supports this dating of the book by adding a sentence not present in the original Hebrew text. It names Jeremiah, a prophet of the sixth century B.C.E., as the book's author: "And it came to pass, after Israel was taken captive and Jerusalem made desolate, that Jeremiah sat weeping, and lamented this lamentation over Jerusalem and said. . . . "

Until recently, interpreters confidently dated the book to the same period, sometime after Jerusalem's fall to the Babylonians and before the end of the exile of some of Jerusalem's citizens to Babylon (587-537). But some scholars challenge the traditional dating (Provan 10-15; O. Kaiser 300-302; and Westermann 1994, 68-76). Provan points out, for example, that Lamentations contains no names or events to anchor it to that time. Its language is allusive and metaphoric rather than historically precise (Mintz), and it describes events in poetic rather than concrete historic terms (but see Dobbs-Allsopp 1998). Provan's refreshing historical skepticism reminds us that poetic works are not trapped in the historical worlds that produced them, and that they take on multiple other meanings in new historical contexts.

But even if Lamentations cannot be secured unquestionably to the Babylonian period, the massive tragedies of that time illumine the book, even if only by analogy. If not this historical catastrophe, then some similar invasion, some parallel disruption of human life, gave birth to this poetry. For that reason the presumed history of that time—a long history of pain, disruption, and death—is helpful for understanding the book. It enables us to imagine the turmoil and loss in which the people lived who produced the book.

Occupation and Exile

The period of Babylonian control (597-537 B.C.E.) was one of immense turmoil and tragedy for the people of Judah and its principal urban center, Jerusalem. Even prior to the three Babylonian attacks on the city, Egypt and Babylon struggled for control of Judah, creating an internal climate of fear and confusion. Babylon eventually defeated Egypt and, in 597, invaded Jerusalem, placed a puppet king on the Judean throne, and deported some of the leading citizens to Babylon. After ten years of uneasy quiet, the king rebelled and provoked a devastating second invasion.

According to biblical accounts, the 587 invasion of Judah devastated the city (2 Kings 24:18-25:26; Jer 39:1-10; 52:1-30; 2 Chr 36:11-20). The siege lasted nearly two years, and the trapped citizenry fought Nebuchadnezzar's armies as well as famine in the walled, isolated city. When the Babylonian forces finally broke through the walls, they destroyed the temple and the king's palace, captured the king, and deported more of the populace to Babylon. Even then, further destruction and turmoil were to follow. When surviving members of the Judean royal family assassinated the Babylonian-appointed governor Gedeliah (Jer 40:1-41:18), the Babylonians invaded a third time and exiled still more people.

Survivors in Jerusalem, where Lamentations was probably written, would likely have been benumbed by years of violence and by deaths of family members. Next they had to cope with scarcity, insecurity, and oppression under foreign occupation. The destruction of political, commercial, and domestic life was immeasurable (Smith-Christopher). Although Lamentations contains oblique references to these aspects of the tragedy, Provan is correct. The poems could come from any of several invasions of Jerusalem. But many traditional associations tether Lamentations to this period, and the book cries out in the midst of conditions like these.

Narrative Wreckage

Along with the destruction of buildings, families, and communal life came the painful collapse of the community's symbolic world, that is, the story of its relationship with God. To borrow a phrase from Arthur Frank (54), the people's story underwent "narrative wreckage." Frank studies stories of cancer survivors. A cancer survivor himself, he talks about the wreckage of one's life story that accompanies the discovery that one has a catastrophic illness. The life one expected to lead, the work one hoped to do, the grandchildren one looked forward to nurturing all disappear from the approaching horizon. That assumed story is over, but a new one has not taken its place and may never do so.

Lamentations plays havoc with the story of Judah's relationship with God. The fall of the city marks the people's abandonment by the God who rescued them from slavery and brought them to the land of promise. That God has turned against them and left them bereft. If God rescues, liberates, and protects as their cherished biblical story tells them, how could such events occur? If God dwells with them in the Jerusalem temple, if God makes covenants with them to be their God, then how could these things happen? Even worse, why did God do these things to them? Like a marriage after a bitter, unanticipated divorce, their shared story is in splinters, and there is no new story to replace it. The people's symbolic world collapsed with the buildings (Stulman). Lamentations depicts that wreckage.

The Marriage of Form and Content

Contemporary artist Ann Bryan writes,

> Art does not answer the impossible theological questions. When thought and reason come to an end in the face of unthinkable evil or unbearable personal loss, art provides us with the means to invent, to organize, to create a place of being where we are helped to endure the question: Where is God? (Bryan 8)

Unthinkable evil and loss come to voice in Lamentations, and there they receive "structure and vitality that can be taken back into the body and re-experienced with understanding that is spiritual and visceral" (Bryan 8).

Art in general and poetry in particular acquire transforming power from the way they marry content with formal or structural features (Yates 17-24). Lamentations is a complex and provocative work of art that draws on traditional forms and harnesses them to the expression of grief, pain, and doubt as a means of survival (Linafelt 2000). Its formal features and poetic devices include:

- multiple poetic voices,
- a mixture of literary genres of complaint and mourning,
- acrostic and alphabetic structures,
- varied lengths of poems,
- personification of the city,
- vibrant, interwoven language and imagery.

With these and other features, Lamentations creates an alchemy of grief, mourning, and despair, turning them into an assertion of life, a kind of survivors' gold. By using and adapting traditional forms, the poems express and embody the content. The forms call forth feelings, ideas, and experiences that make the poetry "more encompassing, more fully engaging, than simply rational reflection" (Yates 19). Even before we attend to the content of the poem, the forms present the voice of suffering, a "sustained *cri de coeur*" (Wallace 33). They help to build this house for sorrow.

More than anything, Lamentations is a book of shifting poetic voices, spoken by partially drawn poetic personae or characters (Lanahan). The voices give the book immense dramatic power and draw us into their experience.

There are two speakers in each chapter, except for the last where only the community speaks. The other speakers include one, or perhaps two, narrators, the personified city called Daughter Zion, and an unidentified male whom I call "the strongman." The voices overlap and contradict each other with passionate, authoritative testimonies about the disasters they have survived. Together they produce an oratorio of sorrows with each voice contributing a partial perspective, an intense but limited testimony about the evil that has engulfed them. The voices conflict with each other and reach no resolution. They yearn for God's voice, but God's voice is missing from the book.

Mixture of Literary Genres

The principal genre or literary form of Lamentations is the lament, but laments come in several types that converge in Lamentations. Laments are prayers that erupt from wounds, burst out of unbearable pain, and bring it to language. Laments complain, shout, and protest. They take anger and despair before God and the community. They grieve. They argue. They find fault. Without complaint there is no lament form. Although laments appear disruptive of God's world, they are acts of fidelity. In vulnerability and honesty, they cling obstinately to God and demand for God to see, hear, and act.

Laments are prayers of the discontented, the disturbed, and the distraught. They protest God's rule of the world, bemoan the speakers' physical conditions, and whine about enemies. But remarkably, in the process of harsh complaint and resistance, they also express faith in God in the midst of chaos, doubt, and confusion. They cry out that life is unbearable, suffering too great, and the future hopeless. The lament forms themselves alert readers that, no matter the complaint, the poems emerge from profound "disorientation" to life (Brueggemann 1984, 51-121).

Laments are common in the Bible and comprise one-third of the psalms. Lamentations adapts the typical lament form by leaving out features in a signal of its own purposes. Typically, laments place emotional extremes right next to each other in seeming contradiction, rapidly shifting from deep unhappiness to heights of confident hope and anticipated joy. Here are typical elements of the lament:

1. Direct address to God
2. Complaint
3. Words that reassure the speaker
4. Motivation for God to act on behalf of the speakers

5. Petition for justice or vengeance
6. Vow or promise to praise (Baumgartner 19-40; Westermann 1981, 64; Ferris 91-92).

Of course, few literary forms exist in their pure state (Frye 18). Instead, writers choose among traditional elements, amending forms to their purposes. The poems in Lamentations stretch the lament form to its limits. They reduce or omit features expressing confident hope, assurance, and praise, and they greatly expand the complaints. Discontent and disorientation abound in the very structure of the poetry itself (Hillers xxvii).

Lamentations draws from features of both individual and communal laments and of laments over the fallen city. Individual laments contain the voice of one person, who uses first-person singular pronouns and possessive forms (I, me, my; Lam 1, 2, and most of 3 and 4), and communal laments speak in the voice of the community, which uses first-person plural forms (we, us, our; Lam 3:40-47; 4:17-22; all of 5; Ferris). But the entire book functions as a specific type of lament, called "lament over the fallen city."

Lamentations bewails the destruction of Jerusalem and God's involvement in it. It is startling to realize that devastations of cities occurred so often in the ancient world that a particular type of lament arose to commemorate and cope with the wreckage and its aftermath. Whether by military attack or by catastrophic natural event, the destruction of a city was and remains a horrific set of events. It overturns human life, destroys human habitats, violates the earth, and kills body and spirit. "Death has come up into our windows," writes Jeremiah about impending Babylonian invasion (Jer 9:21, NRSV).

Borrowed from Israel's neighbors, city laments contain numerous features that occur in or are modified for Lamentations (Dobbs-Allsopp 1994, 30-96; Ferris 157-59; Gwaltney). These include common motifs such as descriptions of destruction, a mournful mood, shifting voices, reversals of fortune, a weeping female figure—usually a goddess representing the city—and complaints of divine abandonment (Dobbs-Allsopp 1993, 39-96). The presence of the form in Lamentations alerts us to the tragedy and sorrow of its speakers.

Lamentations grafts onto this mixture of laments cries known as funeral dirges. A dirge proclaims a death, announces a funeral, and summons the community to mourn (Westermann 1994, 8-11). Lamentations opens with a dirge: "How *('ēkāh)* lonely sits the city once great with people!" (Lam 1:1), and chapters 2 and 4 begin with same mournful cry of "How!" A hybrid combination of forms, the book itself functions as a dirge for the destroyed city, announcing its death, calling for commemoration and inviting mourning.

In keeping with its mixture of sorrowful genre, poems of Lamentations follow a rhythmic beat called *qinah* or "limping" meter, though not consistently and not audibly in English. The *qinah* uses three long and two short beats per line. Its presence in Lamentations is one more way the book expresses and embodies its content, one more way the poetry gives "formfulness" to grief (Brueggemann 1995).

Acrostic and Alphabetic Puzzles

Lamentations is built in varying and intriguing ways upon the Hebrew alphabet. Although not evident in most English translations (*The New Jerusalem Bible* is an exception), the first four poems are acrostics, and the final poem is called "alphabetic." An acrostic is a composition that begins with the first letter of the alphabet and uses the rest of the letters sequentially. Each verse of Lamentations' acrostics begins with consecutive letters of the Hebrew alphabet, but, adding complexity to the poetry, the acrostics vary in length and type. The final poem is "alphabetic" in the sense that it contains twenty-two lines, the same number of lines as the number of consonants in the Hebrew alphabet.

The use of the acrostic form raises interpretive questions. Why write poetry of sorrow in alphabetical order, and why use different alphabetic and acrostic structures? Because it may be easier to grasp the book's alphabetic arrangements visually than to read about them in the abstract, I begin with a diagram of the poems, then I describe them, and finally I raise questions about meanings and relationships among them. The lettered and blank lines signify acrostic shape.

The acrostics of chapters 1 and 2 are the same. Each of twenty-two verses contains three lines, making a poem of sixty-six lines. Only the first word of the verse in these two chapters begins with the appropriate alphabetic letter. Chapter 3 also contains sixty-six lines, but each line is a verse. The poem intensifies the acrostic because it devotes three verses to each alphabetic letter. Three verses begin with "a" (*'alep*, 3:1-3), three with "b" (*bet* 3:4-6), and so forth.

When we get to chapter 4, we expect another heightened acrostic like the one in chapter 3, or perhaps one that further amplifies the form, or one that parallels the acrostics in chapters 1 and 2. The latter arrangement would create a symmetrical frame around chapter 3. But we do not expect the shortened acrostic that we find. Chapter 4 does resemble chapters 1 and 2 because it also contains multiple lines of which only the first word follows the acrostic scheme. But it differs from them because it contains only twenty-two verses of two lines each to make a poem of forty-four lines. Whereas chapter 3 intensifies the original acrostic, chapter 4 diminishes it.

Finally, chapter 5 abandons the acrostic form altogether. It contains only twenty-two lines and has no alphabetic arrangement. But because the number of consonants in Hebrew is twenty-two, the final poem relates to the alphabet by virtue of its length.

Chapter 1
acrostic
22 verses of three lines each, one verse per letter (66 lines)

a _____
_____
_____
b _____
_____
_____

Chapter 2
acrostic
22 verses of three lines each, one verse per letter (66 lines)

a _____
_____
_____
b _____
_____
_____

Chapter 3
acrostic
66 verses of one line each with three verses per letter (66 lines)

a _____
a _____
a _____
b _____
b _____
b _____

Chapter 4
acrostic
22 verses of two lines each (44 lines)

a _____
_____
b _____
_____

Chapter 5
not an acrostic
22 verses of one line each (22 lines)

_____

Pain and Loss in Alphabetic Order

Why does Lamentations use acrostic and alphabetic forms, and how do these unevenly structured poems relate to one another? Interpreters offer several suggestions about the meaning of the alphabetic structures and about the puzzling relationships among the poems. I think the alphabetic devices embody struggles of survivors to contain and control the chaos of unstructured pain, and the variations among the poems reflect the processes of facing their deadening reality.

To write an acrostic is difficult in any language, requiring verbal fluency beyond demands of ordinary poetry. Lamentations' acrostics indicate that the poems are not spontaneous outbursts but carefully composed works.

They separate the poems from one another into separate units, giving space and attention to the voices within them. At the same time, they link the poems and the voices to each other by using common alphabetic devices (Grossberg 84-86).

Acrostics may have functioned as an aid to memory, a mnemonic device from early stages of composition or to help in oral performances in liturgies. But if so, why are there so few acrostics in the Hebrew Bible (Pss 9-10, 25, 34, 119, 145; Na 1; Prv 31:10-31; Soll), even though many poems had oral beginnings and liturgical uses? Besides, acrostics imply writing authors who know the alphabet more than oral composers who need not (Gottwald 1954, 23-32).

Lamentations' alphabetic devices are deeply symbolic. They expose the depth and breadth of suffering in conflicting ways. The alphabet gives both order and shape to suffering that is otherwise inherently chaotic, formless, and out of control. It signifies the enormity of suffering as a vast universe of pain, extending from "A to Z," to which nothing more can be added (Grossberg 84). It tries to force unspeakable pain into a container that is familiar and recognizable even as suffering eludes containment. It implies that suffering is infinite, for it spans the basic components of written language from beginning to end.

Relationships among Chapters

But if alphabetic devices are symbolic, why are the poems of different lengths, and why does the acrostic shrink and disappear? Why does chapter 4 grow shorter than its prototype in chapters 1 and 2? Why is chapter 5 shorter still and not an acrostic? Does the intensified acrostic in chapter 3, the only chapter with sustained words of hope, signal the theological heart of the book? Earlier biblical scholars assumed that the book contained poetic fragments later joined together in a loose anthology in which unevenness among the poems was more or less accidental. But I join those interpreters today who find literary purpose in the book's arrangement (Dobbs-Allsopp, forthcoming; Provan; Hillers; Linafelt 2000; Salters).

Too often interpreters of Lamentations treat the hopeful chapter 3 as though it contained the book's only significant material (Linafelt 2000, 5-13). There are literary reasons to think it is the book's most important chapter, the book's theological heart. It forms the physical center of the poetry, intensifies the acrostic form, and, in lyric cadences its male voice, alone among the book's voices, expresses hope. But this poetry of hope does not conclude the book (Dobbs-Allsopp, forthcoming). Instead, the two final chapters move back to themes of grief, anger, and despair, and smother hope like a blanket over a fire. The shortening poems and shrinking alphabetic forms imply exhaustion, increasing numbness, and the loosening of structures to sustain confidence in God and the future. The forms echo the voices of survivors and imply that despair and doubt have silenced hope or, more likely, coincide with it.

Multiple Testimonies

The complex forms and multiple voices of Lamentations suggest a performance in which multiple speakers offer testimony (Lee). Testimonies are partial statements of truth, told from a limited angle, from a particular contextual space (Chopp 2000). Each poem and each voice of Lamentations stands on its own, expresses one perspective among survivors, but no speaker dominates the other. The book leaves voices and viewpoints unsettled, unresolved, and open-ended. Neither the hope of chapter 3 nor the rage and encroaching despair of the other chapters refutes or triumphs over the other. Together the voices express complex and uneven processes of coping with trauma in which hope flares up and fades. Whether it will return again, no survivor knows for certain, and in Lamentations no arbiter comes to settle the matter.

The City as Woman

One of the book's more effective rhetorical devices is its personification of Jerusalem in chapters 1 and 2. It portrays the city as a woman and calls her by the traditional title "Daughter Zion." Naomi Seidman (285) refers to Zion with the apt epithet "city woman" because sometimes the poetry focuses on her female roles—widow, mother, lover, and rape victim—and sometimes it puts her city features—walls, buildings, and streets—in the foreground. By making Jerusalem a woman, the poetry gives her personality and human characteristics that evoke pity or disdain from readers (Mintz 3-4). Her female body is the object of disgrace and shaming, and her infidelities become shocking, intimate betrayals.

Zion refers to the holy mountain of God's dwelling, the place of the temple. The title "daughter (of)" comes from the ancient Near Eastern practice of referring to the patron goddess of the city as its daughter (Dobbs-Allsopp 1995, 455). Hebrew poetry largely removes goddess language from Zion's lineage, but she remains a potent literary persona and a rare example of a female biblical figure who speaks, resists, and takes a theological position. At first she appears to be a recalcitrant sinner and pathetic figure, but soon she articulates her experience of her life and of her God. Hers is the first and most passionate voice of resistance in the book.

The Missing Voice

The one thing about which all the book's speakers agree is that God must respond to them in their suffering. God must see, pay attention, and remember them. God must take into the divine consciousness the overwhelming destitution in which they live. Only in chapter 3 does God respond, and only briefly in quoted, remembered speech of the past, not directly (Lam 3:57). God's voice is missing, and the book is God-abandoned. But primarily because God is silent, Lamentations expresses human experiences of abandonment with full force. And because God never speaks, the book honors voices of pain. Lamentations is a house for sorrow because there is no speech for God.

Authorship

Ancient Israel was not concerned about authorship as are we, who focus on the individual creativity and ownership of written material with copyrights and lawsuits. Written compositions gained authority in the ancient world not because they were novel and original but quite the opposite. They had authority because they were traditional, or claimed to be so, showing their truth to be grounded in the wisdom and experience of the past. This may explain how the sixth-century prophet Jeremiah came to preside over the book (Lee), even if he was not its author.

In the prophetic book named after him, Jeremiah embodies the community's tears. He is the chief lamenter, who weeps over the fate of his people, laments their failure to repent, and rails against God, whom he accuses of betraying him. Like the man in Lamentations 3:52-53, Jeremiah laments, speaks in captivity, is imprisoned in a pit, and cries out to God for rescue (Jer 38:1-13). The association of Jeremiah with Lamentations is, therefore, not surprising.

But Lamentations' author or authors are unknown. Anonymous poets and survivors of the destruction produced it. Because the book of Jeremiah (41:4-5) tells of citizens going to the site of the destroyed temple to offer sacrifices, some scholars imagine it to be the place where the book took form in worship that continued at the devastated site (Blenkinsopp).

Places in the Canon and Titles

Greek and Hebrew versions of the Bible locate Lamentations in different canonical order and give it different titles. In the Septuagint (Greek translation), Lamentations follows the book of Jeremiah, making further connections between the two books; in the Hebrew or Masoretic Text (MT),

Lamentations occurs among the five liturgical scrolls, called the *megilloth*. The Greek title for the book is *Threni*, or lamentation, from which comes the book's English title. In the Hebrew Bible, however, books receive their titles from the book's first words. The Hebrew name of Lamentations is *Seper 'Ēkāh* ("The Book of How").

Musical Appropriations

Musicians have used lyrics from Lamentations for liturgical pieces and for more general compositions. In the sixteenth century, Thomas Tallis set "The Lamentations of Jeremiah" to music; and in the twentieth century, Pablo Casals composed *O Vos Omnes*, known in English as "O Ye People." For the Lent of 1956, Hungarian composer Lajos Bardos wrote a musical setting for eight verses of chapter 5 to lament national shame, entrapment, and guilt during the Soviet occupation of Hungary. Leonard Bernstein wrote a "Jeremiah" Symphony that uses Lamentations, and Igor Stravinksy composed *Threni* in 1958.

Although Polish composer Henryk Gorecki's "Symphony of Sorrow" (Symphony No. 3) has no direct connection with Lamentations, the symphony is a haunting lament. Its lyrics of great sadness come from testimony scratched on a prison wall and from a mother's lament for her disappeared child. In the exquisite sorrow of the music, this work expresses communal heartbreak at unspeakable horrors of the twentieth century. The work's surprising popularity among music lovers in the United States bears witness to the stored-up grief and unspoken despair in this culture. My book addresses this despair.

2

There Is No One to Comfort You

Lamentations 1

Lamentations opens upon a universe of sorrow. Two speakers, the personified city and an unidentified narrator, draw us into a world of pain, loss, and abandonment. Speaking first, the narrator is unemotional; he coolly describes the city woman's plight and is obsessed with her lost glory (Lam 1:1-11b, 17). By contrast, emotion overwhelms Daughter Zion, who complains only of her present pain, especially the loss of her children (Lam 1:9c, 11c-22). But both speakers recognize her isolation as a factor in her suffering: she "has no one to comfort her" (1:2, 7, 9, 16, 17, 21).

The absence of someone to comfort the city woman haunts the first two poems, and the question of a comforter lingers across the book. But how is comfort possible in the world these poems create? Who or what could comfort this pitiful figure in such extreme conditions? Chapter 1 contains no words of comfort and seems to dismiss its very possibility. Instead, the chapter and the book present pain (Linafelt 2000, 25), and in doing so unexpectedly serve as Zion's comforter, but how this happens does not become clear until chapter 2.

Although the narrator is the book's first speaker, he does little to draw attention to himself here. He is a distant observer, an "objective" reporter who tells us what he sees, but he does not speak to her. His distance and lack of passion contribute to her abandonment. He knows all about her—her glorious past, her grim present, and how she came to her sorry state. By speaking first, he convinces us to accept his perspective on Zion's suffering. He thinks she brought it upon herself.

Daughter Zion uses first person speech (I, me, my) to tell of suffering from the inside, and she speaks not to the narrator but to God. Completely absorbed in her pain, she ignores her past to speak only of the awful now from which she cannot emerge. The immediacy of her speech as victim gives her the moral authority of the survivor and undermines the narrator's perspective. Together the narrator and Daughter Zion testify to a world of horror, chaos, and unmitigated grief. They map Zion's suffering from inside and out to reveal the contours of destroyed life and shattered humanity. They express what Wendy Farley (53) calls "radical suffering," massive and intense suffering that assaults personhood.

Chapter 1 gives both speakers equal opportunity. Their speeches are nearly equal in length, and each interrupts the other to create two balanced panels of poetry (1:1-11b; 1:11c-22).

The Narrator's View of Zion's Fall

To show how the Hebrew text interweaves words across lines and verses in a tight braid of pain, my translation repeats words and avoids synonyms. The names of the Hebrew letters in the margins show the poem's acrostic structure. In this chapter, only the first word of each verse is acrostic.

'*Alep* 1:1 How lonely sits the city once great with people!
She has become like a widow, she who was once great among the nations.
A princess among the provinces, she is now in forced labor.[1]

Bet 1:2 Bitterly she weeps in the night and her tears are upon her cheeks.
There is no one to comfort her among all her lovers.
All her friends have betrayed her; they have become her enemies.

Gimmel 1:3 Judah has gone into exile with affliction and hard servitude.[2]
She dwells among the nations and finds no rest.
All her pursuers overtake her in the midst of her distress.[3]

Dalet 1:4 The roads of Zion are mourning from lack of those who come to the feasts.
All her gates are desolate; her priests are groaning;
Her virgins grieve, and to her it is bitter.

He 1:5 Her foes have become [her] head; her enemies prosper
because YHWH has caused her suffering for her many transgressions.
Her suckling infants went into captivity before the foe.

---

[1] Gordis 1974b, 129; Hillers 1.
[2] Provan 38.
[3] Provan 39; but see Hillers 7.

Waw 1:6   And departed from Daughter Zion is all her splendor.
           Her princes have become like stags that do not find pasture.
           They went without strength before the pursuer.

Zayin 1:7 Jerusalem remembers the days of her affliction and her wandering,
           all her precious things that were from the days of old.
           When her people fell by the hand of the foe and there was no one to help her,
           Her enemies saw her and laughed at her collapse.[4]

Het 1:8   Jerusalem has sinned grievously; therefore, she has become an unclean thing.
           All who honored her make light of her, for they see her nakedness.
           Indeed,[5] she herself groans and turns away.

Tet 1:9   Her uncleanness is on her skirts; she did not remember her future.
           She has fallen terribly.[6] There is no one to comfort her.
           YHWH, look at my affliction for the enemy has made himself great.

Yod 1:10   The foe has spread out his hand upon all her precious things.
           For she has seen nations coming into her sanctuary,
           whom you commanded, "They will not go into your assembly."

Kap 1:11   All her people are groaning, seeking bread.
           They give their precious things for food to stay alive.
           YHWH, look and pay attention for I have become worthless!

With the alarming cry of a funeral dirge, the narrator demands our attention in the poem's opening verse. "How (*'ēkāh*) lonely sits the city once great with people!" (1:1a). The "how" is a bitter declaration that death has occurred, but as Naomi Seidman (283) observes, it also implies interrogation—"How could this happen to beloved Zion?" "How is it possible even to speak of this destruction?" To convey the breath-stopping shock of the catastrophe, Seidman proposes the opening *'ēkāh* "be pronounced with a catch in the throat." Tragedy threatens to overcome speech, sobs interfere

---

[4] Hillers 2. This is the only four-line verse in the chapter. The additional line may be the result of scribal glossing, different textual versions, or simply poetic variation. Efforts to eliminate a line have not met consensus. See Gottlieb's (13) elimination of the third line, for example.

[5] Provan (45) argues that the normal meaning of *gam*, "also," "too," "indeed," makes the most sense here, meaning that even she joins her enemies in despising herself. See Gottlieb 14.

[6] Provan (45); Hillers (2) translates more literally, "she came down astonishingly."

with words, and trauma pounds back expression as the book's voices hover in tension between life-denying silence and the life-giving urge to speak.

The narrator's words point to Zion, as if he has just come upon her and is shocked at her transformation. The city, once "great with people," swollen with life like a pregnant woman, is now alone like a widow (1:1b). The widow in ancient Israel was truly alone. The term refers to a woman who has not only lost her husband but who also lacks children and extended family to support and protect her. She lives on the fringes of society and faces great dangers (Hiebert). This city woman sits on the knife-edge between death and survival.

The contrast between Zion's former greatness and her current slavery makes her loss of freedom conspicuously painful. Once she was a princess, but now she is a slave forced to labor for others (1:1c). Previously elegant, beloved, and honored, she is the conquered slave of another people. The narrator's references to her past sharpen the perception of present sorrows that replace past glories.

Initially, the narrator speaks of Zion from afar, as a sorrowful still life (1:1), but then his words bring her close and she comes to life with bitter tears (1:2a). In her endless days and nights of weeping, "There is no one to comfort her!" (1:2b). The absence of a comforting presence seems as significant to the narrator as her weeping, but who could possibly allay this grief? The candidates for the role of comforter show how hopeless her quest for a comforter is, and their very mention casts aspersions on her character. "Among all her lovers," there is no one to comfort her (1:2b).

Behind this vignette of a woman with false lovers lies the biblical metaphor of God's broken family (O'Connor 1999; Weems). In prophetic portrayals of Israel's infidelity (Hos 1-3; Jer 2:1-4:2), Israel and Judah appear as unfaithful wives. They abandon their divine husband for other gods, false lovers. Daughter Zion is YHWH's unfaithful wife Judah, now conceived of more narrowly as the capital city, cast off and abandoned (Jer 2:1-3:10; Diamond and O'Connor).

Lamentations is, in part, a poetic account of the ruptured relationship between YHWH and Jerusalem. The book does not dwell on the history of that broken marriage because it is concerned with the unspeakable pain of the present. In ancient Israel, a woman's dalliance with lovers branded her a harlot, a sinner, a disreputable person. When the narrator tells of the failure of Zion's lovers to comfort her, his opinion of her is clear. She deserves no comfort, for she has brought her suffering upon herself, and now she is alone.

As Zion sits weeping, the nation of Judah goes into exile and servitude (1:3). In some ways Judah and Zion refer to the same realities of land and people but with the geographic breadth of the nation or with the geographical narrowness of the capital city. Here the narrator distinguishes between Judean exiles sent away and survivors remaining in Zion. The exiles are oppressed, cast out among the nations, and overtaken by pursuers (1:3), but the grim conditions facing Zion remain the narrator's primary concern.

Zion's grief is pervasive, vivid, and palpable as mourning overcomes her (1:4). Grief is a living force permeating the city so thoroughly that even inanimate features like roads, gates, and walls mourn despondently. The city mourns because its people no longer come to worship during the appointed feasts (1:4). Because the temple on Mount Zion is the place of God's dwelling, the loss of worship means the city woman has lost her soul; her priests and virgins groan and grieve. With quiet understatement, the narrator reports Zion's response—"to her it is bitter" (1:4c).

When an unnamed foe surrounds and captures Daughter Zion, her bitter sorrows deepen. The Hebrew verse structure echoes her captivity (1:5). The word "foe" *(ṣār)* occurs at the beginning and end of the verse, linguistically surrounding and capturing Zion and her suffering children just as the foes surround the city. Foes rule over her, wrench her children away, and take them captive. The narrator emphasizes Zion's anguish over her lost children by using the Hebrew "her suckling infants" (*ôlāleyihā*, 1:5c), rather than "sons" (children, *bānîm*), the more common and formal term of parent-child relationship (Linafelt 2000, 49-58). Without her infants, the nursing mother is physically and emotionally bereft, but equally crushing is the narrator's interpretation of why these things have happened. God, he declares, "has caused her suffering for her many transgressions" (1:5b).

Not surprisingly, the narrator accepts the tradition—still common today—that suffering is divine punishment for sin. Several biblical books from Deuteronomy through the prophets teach that disaster and suffering are God's punishment for sin and betrayal (Gottwald 1954, 53-89). In the very next chapter of Lamentations, the narrator will draw back from this theology, often called a "theology of retribution," but in chapter 1 he holds fast to a traditional interpretation of disaster—her suffering is divine punishment for sin.

Zion's loss of glory dominates the narrator's perceptions. For him, the great distance she has fallen from her former splendor magnifies her tragedy (1:6a). He observes that her princes, the pride of Judean manhood, are now weak and powerless before their pursuers (1:6b, c). He imagines that she too longs for her past with its "precious things," but more bitter still is her isolation. When the foes attacked, "there was no one to help her" (1:7).

In the next two verses (1:8-9), the narrator blames her more explicitly. Earlier hints of his disdain become scathing charges against her. Though he calls her "Jerusalem," her city name, her femaleness is uppermost in this climax of shaming accusation (1:8). He accuses her of grievous but unspecified sin that becomes more concrete as he continues. Her sin has made her "unclean" *(nîdāh).* The Hebrew word refers to ritual impurity and can mean "unclean," "impure," or a "mockery" (NRSV). Ritual impurity admits of several interpretations, but its effect is to exclude the unclean person from participation in worship and isolate her from physical contact with others. Among the causes of uncleanness specific to women are menstruation (Lev 15:19-30) and adultery (Num 5:19; O'Connor 1998b, 188; Pham 75).

Menstrual uncleanness becomes part of Daughter Zion's shaming later in this chapter (1:17), but here the narrator implies that she is an adulterer (1:8-9); he has already referred to her lovers (1:2). Her honor has been replaced by shame as former admirers now see her nakedness (1:8b). In ancient Israel, exposure of the body caused profound disgrace, but the city woman's shame may be even more humiliating (Pilch and Malina 119-25). The word translated "her nakedness" *('erwātāh)* may refer specifically to "her genitals" (BDB 788; but see Pham 74). Although the causes of Zion's exposure are not entirely obvious, her degradation dehumanizes her, as her body becomes an object of shame. The narrator describes her response with great simplicity—"she herself groans and turns away" (1:8c).

With careless disregard for her future, "her uncleanness is on her skirts" (1:9a). Perhaps this ambiguous uncleanness refers to menstrual blood, but it is hard to see how it would relate to disregard of the future. More likely, "the uncleanness" of her skirts is evidence of sexual intercourse. The language of physical shaming in these verses is, of course, metaphoric. It is about the city, not the body of a real woman, but it uses the female body as a medium of dishonor and accusation, and by implication blames the city woman for her own fall. And in all this, the narrator observes, "There is no one to comfort her" (1:9b).

Unexpectedly, with no preparation or fanfare, Daughter Zion interrupts the narrator's dispassionate description of her fate. Perhaps his humiliating harangue provoked her to speech. She speaks to God directly and asks for what she wants with commanding speech. "YHWH, look *(rā'āh)* at my affliction for the enemy has made himself great" (1:9c). She demands that God see *(rā'āh).* Her plea, the first of many in the book, is as notable for what it does not ask as for what it does. She does not beg for relief, for vindication, or for restoration. She does not ask for the return of her children, for freedom, or for the return of past splendor. She asks only that God will look, see, take into consciousness what the enemy has done to her. She wants God to see her pain. God does not reply.

Without acknowledging her, the narrator abruptly resumes his speech, but he seems to have been listening, because he too speaks of the invader's success. "The foe has spread out his hand upon all her precious things" (1:10a). The narrator grows perplexed and accusatory as the enemy penetrates the temple in a shocking rape of the city woman (1:10b-c, Linafelt and Dobbs-Allsopp 2001). He confronts God and quotes previous assurances of divine protection. The nations have invaded the sanctuary even though "you commanded, 'They will not go into your assembly'" (1:10c). The narrator leaves the addressee unnamed, but he can be speaking to no one but God, as though he knew God had been listening all along.

For the narrator, Zion's most precious thing is the temple. Foreigners have penetrated it and profaned it; they have brought worship to an end despite divine commands prohibiting even entrance to the temple. The city woman's losses and those of her inhabitants echo one another as they both lose their precious things. Her people are devastated, "groaning, seeking bread," bartering "their precious things" simply to eat (1:11; cf. 10a). But the loss of treasures is not all that is at stake—survival hangs in the balance.

In this opening panel of poetry (1:1-11b), the poetic voice I call the narrator sets the scene for the poem and the book. The city is shamed, devastated, and its people are on the brink of death. The narrator gives little hint of his feelings as he describes the devastation before him. The power of his speech derives from his description of the city as a woman. It is her tears, her humiliation, and her comfortlessness to which he points. Enemies attack her; lovers betray her, expose and humiliate her; and her people have gone into exile.

Inheriting the personified city from ancient Near Eastern texts, and Daughter Zion from the book of Jeremiah, the poet(s) of Lamentations chooses not just any female image but that of a fallen and abandoned woman. She is a woman who is "raped and defiled" but who has survived "as a living witness to pain that knows no release" (Mintz 3). Her violation corresponds to the violation of the sacred temple; both sacred, intimate places are penetrated by a despoiler. From the narrator's perspective, she has caused her own pain by sexual liaisons that express betrayal and violence. Yet the central feature of her pain is only hinted at so far—her separation from and loss of her children (Linafelt 2000, 43-58). In all this she has no comforter.

Daughter Zion Pleads for God to See

Daughter Zion becomes the principal speaker in the second half of the poem (1:11c-22). The poem binds her words to the narrator's by beginning them as the last line of the *kap* stanza, one line short of the poem's halfway mark (1:11c-22). Her words correspond in length to the narrator's, and he interrupts her (1:17) as she did him (1:9c). The acrostic form embraces both speeches, further uniting them. I divide the translation at the end of verse eleven to leave the *kap* stanza (1:11) whole, even though Daughter Zion has already begun speaking.

When Daughter Zion interrupts the narrator a second time, she again ignores him and turns with vehemence and desperation to God. "YHWH, look *(rā'āh)*, and pay attention *(nābaṭ)* for I have become worthless!" (1:11c). She uses the same verb of seeing as she did in 1:9c but now she adds a second verb that intensifies her request, demanding that God "pay attention." Apparently accepting the narrator's interpretation of her guilt, she wants YHWH to see how worthless she has become. Perhaps hidden in her plea is a claim upon YHWH's past devotion to her. If YHWH saw and paid attention to her, if YHWH recognized her state, then maybe YHWH would act on her behalf. When YHWH does not respond, she turns instead to the passersby in the poem's second half.

Lamed 1:12 Is it nothing to you who pass by on the way?[7] Pay attention and look!
    Is there any pain like my pain, which was severely dealt upon me,
    Which YHWH inflicted on the day of his fierce anger?

Mem 1:13 From on high he sent fire, into my bones it came down.[8]
    He spread a net for my feet; he turned me back.
    He left me devastated, faint all day long.

Nun 1:14 My transgressions were bound in a yoke, by his hand they were woven together.[9]
    They weigh on my neck; he made my strength fail.
    Adonai has given me into their hands; I am not able to rise.

Samek 1:15 Adonai[10] made light of all my mighty men in my midst.
    He called against me a feast to break my young men.
    As in a winepress Adonai had trodden virgin Daughter Judah.

---

[7] The first words in the verse are not easy to translate (Provan 48). They can be translated "not for you," meaning "not intended for you" (Westermann 1994, 113). "Is it nothing to you?" Gordis (1974b, 157; cf. NRSV) makes sense of the imperatives in the line's second part.

[8] Following Hillers 11; but see Gordis 1974b, 157.

[9] Provan 14; Freedman 144.

[10] Hillers (12) points out that Adonai, another title for God, occurs fourteen times in Lamentations and the nuances of the shift from YHWH (in 1:14c) are unclear.

'*Ayin* 1:16 For these things I weep; my eye, my eye runs down with tears,
Because my comforter is far from me, one who would turn my spirit.
My children are desolate because the enemy prevailed.

Pe 1:17 Zion spread out her hands; there is no one to comfort her.
YHWH commanded his foes to surround Jacob.
Jerusalem has become a menstrual rag among them.

Sade 1:18 YHWH is in the right for I have rebelled against his word.
Listen, I beg you, all peoples and see my pain.
My virgins and my young men have gone into captivity.

Qop 1:19 I have called to my lovers; they have dealt treacherously with me.
My priests and my elders perished in the city
As they sought food for themselves to revive themselves.

Res 1:20 Look, YHWH, I am in anguish; my bowels are in ferment.
My heart has turned in the midst of me for I have greatly rebelled.
In the street the sword bereaves; in the house it is like death.[11]

Sin 1:21 Hear[12] how I am groaning; there is no one to comfort me.
All my enemies have heard of my wickedness; they exalt because you did it.
You brought the day you proclaimed; let them be like me.

Taw 1:22 Let all their wickedness come before you and deal severely with them
As you have dealt severely with me on account of all my transgressions
For many are my groans and my heart is faint.

When God does not respond to Zion's demand for God to see her suffering, she turns to passersby. *Passersby* is a conventional term in Hebrew poetry for witnesses of suffering and devastation who often mock the sufferer and do not intervene (Provan 48; Albrektson 68; cf. Ps 89:1). Zion may be charging them with indifference, or she may be saying the opposite, meaning "Is it not for you?" (that is, I suffer as warning to you; Provan 48). Whatever the significance of her appeal, she wants them to do what God has failed to do—"pay attention and look" (*nābaṭ* and *rāʾāh*, 1:12a). She uses the same verbs as in 1:11c but in reverse order, interweaving them across stanzas and hammering home by sound and repetition the persistence of her need. She needs someone to see her suffering, to acknowledge it, to attend to it. She urgently needs someone to see!

---

[11] Provan 55; Renkema 192.
[12] Reading as imperative (Hillers 14-15).

She follows her demand to the passersby with a rhetorical question that sounds grandiose—"Is there any pain like my pain which was severely dealt upon me?" (1:12b). The implied answer is "No, there is no pain like yours." But her question is not egotistical; it points to the enormity of her suffering, so far beyond her capacity to absorb that no other can be measured against it. It is suffering that knows no bounds, beyond comparison to other suffering. Her pain is both physical and mental. Whether it can be measured against others' pain or against their disasters is ultimately not the point.

In the face of trauma, catastrophe, and radical suffering, claims of incomparability and uniqueness do not function as equations of measurement. They serve, instead, to express the vastness of pain that overcomes individuals and groups, suffering that defies containment, that blasts away at the imagination, that has no words to express its depth and totality. From her position inside the pain, no one has suffered as much as she because there is no way she could imagine more suffering.

Her suffering "was severely dealt" upon her (1:12b), she claims, using the passive voice that leaves the agent of her pain unnamed. Readers of Hebrew poetry expect in the next line (1:12c) a parallel statement about her pain, another expression of her suffering's overwhelming nature. Instead, Zion utters what Dobbs-Allsopp (2001) calls an "enjambed" line of poetry—a run-over sentence from the previous line. The pain cannot wait for the niceties of poetry; it just blurts out the horrible truth in a rush to confession. The run-over line makes the agent of her pain specific and active. It shocks both by altering the expected pattern of poetry and by its alarming content. It is pain "which YHWH inflicted on the day of his fierce anger."

God's burning anger is the subject of the next three verses (1:13-15). Daughter Zion uses active verbs that pile upon one another in a torrent of violence, and YHWH is the agent of that violence. He set her bones on fire, spread a net for her feet, turned her back. He left her "devastated" (1:13). He yokes her with her own transgressions, treads upon her like grapes in a winepress (1:14-15). His merciless battering leaves her faint and she cannot get up. Her words create a scene of domestic violence in which a powerful, angry man beats his wife, hurls her about, and leaves her for dead. The recognition that God is the batterer compounds her pain.

Reminding us that she has been weeping bitterly since the poem's beginning (1:2), she now tells us why (1:16). She does not weep over matters that distressed the narrator—her former glory, her lost status as a princess, her former position as "great among the nations" (1:1). She weeps because of God's awful treatment of her and because she is unable to get anyone to see, to look, to pay attention. Her weeping is endless. She speaks of her eye twice—"my eye, my eye runs down with tears"—as if wordless weeping itself conveyed all her suffering.

The city woman's weeping spills over into other lines and other causes. In another enjambed line she says that she weeps "because my comforter is far from me, one who would turn my spirit" (1:16b). Her devastation might be borne, she implies, were she to have a comforter. But the final line of the verse gives a still further reason for her tears. The line is not a spill over from the previous one. It is a sentence that stands alone and suggests she can never be comforted: "My children are desolate because the enemy prevailed" (1:16c). The desolation of children means unbearable heartbreak and the loss of a future. In the ancient world, a woman's identity derived from motherhood, and her security was bound to the children's survival and well-being. Both are in jeopardy because "the enemy prevailed."

Abruptly, the narrator interrupts her (1:17). Like a Greek chorus commenting on the action, he describes what he sees. "Zion spread out her hands; there is no one to comfort her" (1:17a). Her gesture is an act of imprecation, an effort to draw someone into her plight—the passersby, the narrator, God (Renkema 176-177). But there is "no one to comfort her," the narrator observes again, echoing her previous statement (1:16b). The narrator agrees with her assessment of her plight—YHWH designed the enemy's attack upon her.

Then he adds a description of her humiliation and shame. "Jerusalem has become a menstrual *(niddāh)* rag among them" (1:17c). The Hebrew word, often translated generically as "unclean thing" (Freedman 147), relates to ritual impurity caused by menstruation and conveys the notion of intimate shame (Lev 12:2, 5; 15:19-33). No members of the Israelite community would touch such a rag for they too would risk becoming ritually impure. To say that Zion has become a menstrual or, euphemistically, a "filthy thing" (NRSV) makes her shame vivid, graphic, and repulsive. It also underscores her isolation—she is untouchable and without a comforter.

Daughter Zion resumes speaking in two verses that focus on her present horrors (1:18-20). Like a woman in an abusive relationship, she agrees that YHWH is justified in his treatment of her because she has "rebelled against his word" (1:18a). She appeals again to others to listen and to see *(rā'āh)* her pain, but now it focuses entirely on the children, "my virgins and my young men who have gone into captivity" (1:18c). Since marriageable young people are exiled, the city's future is smashed and the mother's heart is broken. She admits that she had other lovers who betrayed her when she called to them. Her isolation, pain, and self-blaming increase because the priests and the elders are dying of starvation (1:19).

Typical of lament prayers, she concludes her speech with a petition (1:20-22), and her demands echo earlier ones (1:9c and 11c). She again begs YHWH to "look" *(rā'āh)*. She cannot get God's attention, cannot get God to see her sorrow and desolation, but she must. Her bowels are in torment, her spirit in anguish, her heart disturbed, because it is all her fault; she has "greatly rebelled" (1:20). "Hear how I am groaning," she insists, perhaps reversing Moses' famous command, "Hear, O Israel, the Lord is your God, the Lord alone" (Deut 6:4, NRSV). Her pain and grief should affect God, cause God to act on her behalf because of their covenant loyalty to each other. But God does not act. "There is no one to comfort me" (1:21a).

She imagines that her enemies delight in her brokenness, because YHWH brought the day of judgment upon her. "Let them be like me," she cries (1:21c). "Deal severely with them as you have dealt severely with me" (1:22a, b). Perhaps if YHWH could realize and take into account her enemies' wickedness—"let all their wickedness come before you" (1:22a)—the scales would be balanced.

The deepest need of Zion is for God to see, to become aware of the way events are destroying her. She admits her sinfulness, but she knows her attacking foes are not free of sin either. Her last line in this first poem is a massive understatement—"Many are my groans" (1:22c). Indeed, her heart has every cause to be faint. If only God would look, pay attention, hear, then God might learn how much her world and her life are in chaos. God might change things, might comfort her, or at least, might stop attacking her and destroy her enemies.

A Topography of Pain

The first chapter of Lamentations creates a topography of pain. With two voices it maps the heights and depths, the contours and colors of Daughter Zion's suffering. In symmetrical speeches, the two poetic figures provide different perspectives on her destruction and her woundedness. From the outside, the narrator focuses repeatedly on her losses and reversals of circumstance, on her fall from princess to slave, from fully inhabited city to a lonely widow on a hill. He sees her loss of power, wealth, honor, status, and security. He tells of her betrayal by lovers, the penetration of her temple by the foe, and the devastation of her inhabitants. He blames her for her suffering and remarks on her lack of a comforter. His feelings are not there; he does not expose himself, even as he describes unutterable horrors.

Daughter Zion speaks from within the trauma. Her first-person statements carry the power of experience and the cascading confusion of the survivor. She is immersed in emotions, overwhelmed by horror. Her speech piles disaster upon disaster, and she is barely able to continue. She agrees with the narrator that her destruction is an act of God, who batters and brutalizes her, and she agrees that she must accept blame for her rebellion and infidelity. She grieves over her dying inhabitants and is desperate over her children's plight. She weeps endlessly, her bowels are in ferment, and she groans with no one to comfort her. The narrator has seen well—she, indeed, needs a comforter. She needs someone to see her and to pay attention to her suffering, but there is no one.

As a survivor of trauma, there is no aspect of her body, spirit, or her environment unaffected by the catastrophe. All that could be added is a slow, tortured death, and death would be a release. As a survivor of assault and rape, she becomes a "living witness to a pain that knows no release" (Mintz 3). Although rape hurts women physically and spiritually, and in the ancient world also cut off their futures, rape is not Zion's greatest tragedy. The loss of her children brings far more pain. While her infidelities enable the poetry to blame her, they are not the most significant features of the rhetoric about Zion. Her abandonment, her battering and assault, and the loss of her children evoke greater fear and pity.

Like most survivors of trauma, Daughter Zion cannot get a hearing (Herman 175-181; Frank 101-116). Overriding the many layers of her pain is rejection. The most excruciating and dehumanizing aspect of this poem's rhetoric of grief is that Zion cannot get God or anyone to see her, look at her, or recognize her pain. When she finds words for her pain, she cannot get a hearing. There is no one to comfort her.

3

Your Suffering Is Vast as the Sea

Lamentations 2

Chapter 2 begins in the middle of things; it needs chapter 1 to give it a setting. Without it, chapter 2 would burst upon us like an angry storm, advancing without warning. Daughter Zion's desperate conditions in chapter 1 provide reasons for the accelerating fury of chapter 2. Depending on how we interpret her situation, chapter 1 primes us to lament with her, justify divine punishment of her, or rage against God on her behalf.

Chapter 1 calls us to the city woman's side, even if we have doubts about her character. Without the sympathy for her and the appreciation of her losses that chapter 1 instills, chapter 2 would hang in the air. Its acerbic charges against God, its outrage, and its insistent pleas for justice would lack weight and emotive power. The book's second poem shifts away from the weeping woman toward God, who assaulted her. New details of her abasement do appear in chapter 2, but they emerge primarily from the charges against YHWH rather than from an immediate account of her sufferings. Chapter 2 lays her tragedies at the feet of God.

Just as the speeches in chapter 2 build upon chapter 1, the second poem also follows the same acrostic pattern as the first. It too contains twenty-two verses of three lines each in which the first word of each verse follows consecutive alphabetic order. Also like the first poem, the second poem begins with the cry of *'ēkāh* (how), the dirge-like exclamation expected in a funeral setting. But because the two are acrostics that proceed from *'alep* to *taw* (a to z), they are also self-contained poetic units that can stand alone, and indeed many interpreters have treated chapter 2 that way (Re'emi 91-

92; Westermann 1994, 149-59; Hillers 41; but see Provan 57 and especially Linafelt 2000, 71-119). But formal parallels, identical speakers, and connections of content intimately bind the two poems. The narrator and Daughter Zion appear in both, and the interaction between the two begun in chapter 1 continues here at a higher pitch and with greater intensity.

The narrator's words dominate the second chapter. He is the only speaker for most of it (2:1-19); at the narrator's urging Zion bursts in only in the last two verses (2:20-22). The narrator speaks about and to Zion with third- and second-person singular forms, whereas she speaks of herself in the first-person singular (2:22). She could, therefore, also be the speaker of the first-person lament of verse 11. But since the narrator refers to himself in that way (2:13), and since verse 11 is embedded in his larger speech, he is probably the speaker there too (but see Re'emi 91).

Structure of the Poem

Because the narrator does most of the speaking, chapter 2 does not divide as symmetrically as chapter 1. Instead, there are three panels of poetry, two of which belong to the narrator (2:1-10; 2:11-19) and one to Daughter Zion (2:20-22). In the first poetic panel (2:1-10), the narrator speaks of God's overflowing anger and its effects on Zion. He uses third-person speech across these verses. In the second panel (2:11-19), he tells of his own response to Zion's plight. He speaks about himself for the first time (2:11-13), and he addresses her in second feminine singular forms (2:13-19). When Zion speaks, she addresses God and uses the same imperative verbs she used in the previous chapter (2:20-22).

The Narrator as Participant in Zion's Reality

Although the narrator dominates the poem, his words concentrate on Zion's suffering. But now he no longer speaks as a distant observer; in this chapter he is an overwrought participant in Zion's unbearable reality (Linafelt 2000, 52). Again he addresses us instead of God, but it is God's involvement that obsesses him.

In the Day of God's Anger (Lam 2:1-10)

'Alep 2:1   How Adonai in his anger has set Daughter Zion under a cloud![1]
He has cast down from heaven to earth the honor of Israel.
And he did not remember his footrest on the day of his anger.

---

[1] Re'emi 92.

Bet 2:2   Adonai swallowed up without pity all the dwellings of Jacob.
He threw down in his overflowing rage the fortresses of Daughter Judah.
He brought down to the ground, defiled[2] in dishonor the kingdom and her princes.

Gimmel 2:3 He hewed down in his burning anger all the strength of Israel.
He has turned back his right hand from the face of the enemy.
He has burned against Jacob like a flaming fire, consuming all around.

Dalet 2:4   He has bent his bow like an enemy. He has taken a stand with his right hand like a foe.
He has killed all that was desirable to the eye
in the tent of Daughter Zion. He has poured out his rage like fire.[3]

He 2:5   Adonai has become like an enemy; he has swallowed up Israel.
He has swallowed up all her palaces; he has ruined his fortifications.
He has multiplied in Daughter Judah mourning and mourning.

Waw 2:6   He tore down his booth like a garden,[4] he destroyed his appointed place.
YHWH caused feast and sabbath to be forgotten in Zion.
He spurned in his indignant anger king and priest.

Zayin 2:7   Adonai rejected his altar; he abhorred his sanctuary.
He delivered into the hand of the enemy the walls of her palaces.
They clamored[5] in the house of YHWH as on a feast day.

Het 2:8   YHWH planned to destroy the walls of Daughter Zion.
He stretched out a line; he did not turn his hand from swallowing.
He caused fortress and wall to mourn; together they languished.

Tet 2:9   Her gates have sunk into the ground; he destroyed and shattered her bars.[6]
Her king and her princes are among the nations; there is no Torah.
Indeed, her prophets have not found a vision from YHWH.

Yod 2:10   The elders of Daughter Zion sit upon the ground in silence.
They put dust upon their heads; they put on sackcloth.
The virgins of Jerusalem hang their heads to the earth.

---

[2] Renkema 222.
[3] This verse is ragged in the Hebrew.
[4] Westermann 1994, 144-145.
[5] Following the NRSV, literally "they lifted voice."
[6] Hillers (38) drops the first verb because in Hebrew it seems to overstuff the line.

The narrator begins again with another *'ēkāh* (how; see 1:1 and 4:1) as death engulfs everything. He hurls accusations at God (2:1-8) and tells of the deadly effects of God's assault upon Daughter Zion (2:9-10). His lament contains a ragged, rhythmic account of God's violence against Zion. Verbs of attack and destruction against Zion or her people pile upon one another, and the subject of each is God. God beclouds, casts down, does not remember; God swallows up, does not spare, throws down in rage; God brings to the ground, cuts down, brings back his hand; God burns, bends his bow, kills all, pours out rage.

The verbs accumulate as if the narrator is overcome with his own fury. Anger pours from him in verbal brilliance as he tries to understand the devastation he sees. His interpretation of Zion's predicament changes in this chapter. He no longer blames her; instead, he charges God with violent abuse of city woman Zion.

The first stanza tells why the narrator is so angry (2:1). The one God treats with such brutality is God's special city woman. "How Adonai in his anger has set Daughter Zion under a cloud" (2:1a). God's "beclouding" of Zion means there is a murky barrier between the two, a blocking out, a veiling or erasing of her identity. God can no longer see her or be disturbed by her appearance, once most precious to God. Erasing her identity with a cloud may be necessary for God to treat her as the narrator says he does in this poem. She has been the "honor of Israel," the principal city, residence of the king, and site of God's own dwelling place, God's own "footrest." It is she whom God "casts down from heaven to earth" (2:1b).

Then the narrator begins a hammering description of God's attack on the whole land of Jacob, Judah, Israel, and Jerusalem (2:2-8). But while the narrator depicts the assault on land and people, he is simultaneously charging God with infidelity, lack of integrity, and loss of self-control. God's actions are vicious. God "swallowed up" dwelling places, "threw down fortresses," "brought down to the ground, defiled in dishonor the kingdom and her princes" (2:2). God "hewed down" the strength of Israel; God burned and consumed Jacob (2:3). God has taken up his bow and killed all that was good (2:4). God has become an enemy, and has swallowed up Israel, palaces, and fortifications (2:5). God tore down his booth and spurned king and priest (2:6). God has rejected the altar, abhorred the sanctuary, and delivered Zion's palaces to the enemy (2:7). God planned to ruin Daughter Zion, and he "did not turn his hand from swallowing" (2:8).

In this litany of anti-praises, the narrator points to God's motive for battering Zion. It is anger (2:1), indignant rage, overflowing (2:6), burning, (2:3), destructive as fire (2:4). God is mad, out of control, swirling about in unbridled destruction. God has become an enemy who has destroyed buildings, homes, walls, fortifications, feasts, sabbaths, government, and palaces. These objects of divine fury are metonyms, expressions in which a part stands for the whole. The destroyed city walls mean the destroyed city, since the razing of the walls allows the enemy to enter without resistance. The destruction of the palace means the whole nation's collapse, because the seat of the government is destroyed. The loss of feast and sabbath in Zion means the end of worship in the land. Divine rejection of the altar and hatred of the sanctuary means that God has abandoned the temple, the city, the land, and the people. The world, as the people of Zion know it, has come to an end.

Although the narrator speaks of destructive divine rage akin to an uncontrolled tantrum, more shocking still is the narrator's accusation that God acted out of calculated cruelty. YHWH "planned *(ḥāšab)* to destroy the walls of Daughter Zion" (2:8). The Hebrew verb denotes intention. From the narrator's viewpoint, the attack on the city was not merely an accidental result of momentary passion, but planned and decided with malice and forethought.

The indignant quality of divine anger implies that someone provoked it; God is indignant because Zion sinned. But in this chapter, the narrator barely mentions Zion's moral failures, sexual dalliances, or ritual uncleanness that concerned him in chapter 1 (see 2:14). Instead, her guilt fades from poetic concern, and the narrator's charges are against God alone. It is divine behavior that obsesses him, and God's behavior, not Zion's, is reprehensible.

For the narrator, God's cruel actions contradict God's own interests. God violated God's special relationship with Zion, destroyed God's own dwelling place, and ended the worship in the temple that celebrated and sealed that relationship. God acts against God's own footrest (2:1), appointed place (2:6), altar, and sanctuary and it is in God's own house that the enemy clamored in a mockery of true worship (2:7). God has not protected the people from the enemy but with weapons of war has attacked them.

The abrupt shift in the narrator's focus from Zion's sinfulness to God's cruelty receives no direct explanation, except that it follows Zion's bitter lament in chapter 1. Her words affect him, and she informs the focus of his interpretation as he continues to notice the impact of divine fury upon her. He sees that God has set her under a cloud, swallowed her up without pity (2:1), and killed all "that was desirable" in her tent (2:4b). He sees that God has multiplied mourning in Daughter Zion, as he multiplies it himself by repeating the word "mourning and mourning" (2:5c).

Now the narrator changes focus again from the violence itself to its effects upon Zion and her inhabitants (2:9-10). The city gates, the entryways to the social centers of city life, "have sunk into the ground" (2:9). The earth itself swallowed them, as the divine "swallowing" (2:1, 5, 8) engulfed the city in destruction. Entrance gates are gone; protecting bars are shattered; the city's rulers are dispersed among the nations, and "there is no Torah" (2:9).

Torah refers to the divine law or instruction that seals Israel's covenant with God, provides governing principles of justice and worship, and gives the community its covenanted identity. The Torah showed the people how to live together and to live with God. Its disappearance expresses how total is the nation's collapse. Not only are physical and material things, symbolic buildings, and people's lives destroyed, but the Torah, the beating heart of their life together, has disappeared. And just as there is no Torah instruction by the priests, the prophets have no visions; communication with God is cut off. The prophets have nothing to say to the devastated people, neither to chastise nor to comfort them. The void is enormous, for YHWH has severed relations with them, and the people may have no future at all.

Death and grieving prevail (2:10). Old and young convey sorrow by their posture, their actions, and their silences; elders say nothing as they perform mourning rituals. They put dust on their heads, wear sackcloth, and "sit upon the earth." Young women—virgins on the brink of life, awaiting marriage, motherhood, and the future—hang their heads in grief to "the ground." There is nothing to say, no words to heal by, no hope for life ahead. There is only exhaustion, despair, and the overbearing presence of grief.

God takes everything in a downward direction. God casts down Zion from heaven to the ground (2:1); God throws down in overflowing rage the fortresses of Judah. God "brings down to the ground," defiles in dishonor the kingdom and her princes, "throws down the fortresses and the kingdom and her princes" (2:2). God brings down "to the ground" the city gates, the elders, and the virgins (2:9-10). God hews down (2:3) and tears down (2:6). That which was upright and those who were erect and proud are brought low. Then God swallows up. Living space disappears altogether as God "swallowed up" *(billa')* their dwellings (2:2), "swallowed up *(billa')* Israel" (2:5), and "swallowed up *(billa')* all her palaces" (2:5). There is no space left to live, to be. For the city's inhabitants, there is only the ground upon which to sit in silent pain.

The Narrator's Conversion

Little by little in chapter 2, the narrator drops his dispassionate stance to become wholly engaged in Zion's tragedy. He forgets her guilt and his accusations in chapter 1 and turns furiously against the divine attacker. He stands with her and speaks on her behalf, accusing the God whose beloved she once was of betrayal and abuse, of excessive and calculated rage. In the next panel of poetry, the narrator moves even further from his original indifference toward compassion for Zion.

Weep, Day and Night (2:11-19)

Kap 2:11   My eyes waste with tears; my bowels are in ferment;

      My bile is poured out on the ground because of the breaking of the daughter of my people,

      As the child and the infant are fainting in the streets of the city.

Lamed 2:12 To their mothers they say, "Where is the corn and the wine?"

      As they faint like the mortally wounded in the streets of the city,

      As their lives are poured out on the breasts of their mothers.

Mem 2:13   What can I say for you? What can I compare to you, O Daughter of Jerusalem?

      What can I liken to you that I may comfort you, O Virgin Daughter Zion?

      For great as the sea is your breaking,[7] who can heal you?

Nun 2:14   Your prophets saw empty and vain visions for you.

      They have not uncovered your iniquity to turn away your captivity.

      They have seen for you empty and vain visions.

Samek 2:15 All passersby along the way clap their hands against you.

      They hiss and shake their heads against Daughter Zion.

      "Is this the city that they say is 'the perfection of beauty, the joy of all the earth?'"

Pe 2:16   All your enemies opened their mouths against you.

      They hissed; they gnashed their teeth; they said, "We swallowed you up.

      Ah, this is the day we waited for eagerly. We have found and seen (it)."

'Ayin 2:17 YHWH did what he planned. He accomplished his word

      That he commanded from days of old. He threw down and did not pity,

      And he caused the enemy to rejoice over you; he raised up the strength of your foe.

Sadeh 2:18 Cry out[8] with your heart to Adonai, O wall of Daughter Zion.

      Let tears run down like a torrent day and night.

      Do not let yourself stop; do not let your eyes be still.

---

[7] NIV translates "wound."

[8] Emending to the imperative with the MT correction (Hillers 40-41).

Qop 2:19 Arise, cry out in the night at the head of the watches.
            Pour out your heart like water before the face of Adonai.
            Lift up your hands to him concerning the life of your children who are
                fainting at the head of every street.

In this second panel of poetry (2:11-19), everything changes. The narrator's own response to Zion's wounds becomes part of his lament (2:11-13). For the first time, he speaks to her directly (2:13-19). He tries to explain why these things happened (2:14, 17) and how badly outsiders behaved (2:15, 16). Then he gives her advice (2:18, 19), and his tone moves from rage against God to empathy for her. His altered attitude could hardly be more remarkable in view of his cool, unengaged stance in chapter 1. Now Zion's pain affects him so deeply that it becomes his as well.

No longer an observer lacking any semblance of personal response, the narrator is so affected by Zion's suffering that he is ill. His body responds to her trauma. To speak of his inner world he uses conventional imagery from the Psalms, but his language is vivid. His eyes "waste with tears," his gut wrenches, and perhaps he is vomiting because his "bile is poured out on the ground" (2:11). The horrors of her life break in on him, and he witnesses to the "breaking *(šeber)* of the daughter of my people." The city woman is broken, wounded, and shattered as he has described, but now he himself moves into her lonely, comfortless space, and her realities engulf him.

The narrator now turns to an aspect of Daughter Zion's suffering that he has noticed only minimally—the plight of her children. Linafelt (2000, 56) thinks the fate of the children finally and definitively moves the narrator. As a poetic image, the sight of mothers watching their babies die is the most heart-wrenching of disasters. By contrast, Mintz (24) argues that the most effective rhetorical way to convey the pain of the fallen city woman is to portray her as a survivor of rape, because her pain and shame never end. But Mintz is wrong; a far more devastating scenario for most women is to watch the suffering and death of their children.

In the ancient world, women's very identity, sense of worth, and place in family and society depended upon offspring. Not only were women bonded to their children physically and emotionally, but women's future security hinged upon survival of sons who would support them in old age. Lamentations uses these cultural realities to describe the city woman's fate. Without children to populate the city, Zion has no future.

When her children faint in the streets, Daughter Zion's "breaking" is complete (2:11). The children ask their mothers for food as they die upon their mothers' breasts (2:12). Their deaths, taking place in public view on the streets of the city, and the sight of other children fainting around him bring the narrator to tears and reveal the unfathomable depths of Daughter Zion's suffering. He has entered her space, her world, her horror; he *sees*.

The narrator's questions reveal both his helplessness and his comprehension of her suffering: "What can I say for you?" "What can I compare to you?" "Who can heal you?" Answers are implied in the questions: There is nothing to say; nothing can compare to you; no one can heal you. Nothing is adequate to express her pain, for her suffering is beyond compare, unspeakable, unhealable, and greater than the sea itself. Perhaps if the narrator could find a comparable reality to her suffering, he would be able to limit it, contain it, somehow make it manageable, put limits around it, bind it off from infinity, and offer her comfort.

A comparison might make her suffering like some other. A comparison might contain it in a space, a time. A comparison might give it metaphorical restraint at least. But her suffering is beyond compare, so its beginnings and endings are not visible, not even imaginable. It stretches beyond sight the way the vast sea stretches endlessly downward and outward beyond visible horizons and measurable depths.

Perhaps the narrator's comparison with the sea is a preposterous overstatement. After all, he does what he says cannot be done—he compares her pain to something else. But the poetry only appears exaggerated and hyperbolic if we take it literally. His comparison to the endless, chaotic, uncontrollable sea—and to the ancients, nearly boundless—makes the point. Daughter Zion's pain is gargantuan, unspeakable. Nothing can be added to it for it stretches infinitely, wildly, and with no limits in sight. Her "breaking," her wound, and the despair they produce pour endlessly into the future. "Who can heal you?" The only possible healer is God, but God is the very one who assaulted her and smashed her in the first place.

Now the narrator speaks to Daughter Zion, for the first time in the book, as if he finally recognizes her humanity (2:13). So far he has only spoken about her, described her, been numbed by her conditions. Now he addresses her with dignifying epithets—he calls her "Daughter of Jerusalem" and then "Virgin Daughter Zion." Of course, both are traditional titles for the city, but here he adds "virgin" *(bĕtûlat)* to the title. The Hebrew term means an unmarried woman of marriageable age. For her to be marriageable in the ancient world indicates that she is a virgin.

When the narrator calls Zion virgin has he forgot her own admission in chapter 1 that she had many lovers (1:19)? Or does his use of the term show that she may be innocent, not as responsible for her suffering as he once thought? Is God so out of hand that her guilt is insignificant by comparison? Jeremiah (31:21) also uses virgin as a title for the city and the country and conveys a similar "re-virginizing" of the former harlot. Here, the term is one of endearment and respect as the narrator seeks to comfort her.

Provan (73) thinks the narrator fails in his effort to comfort Zion, for how can she be comforted in this extremity of loss? Surely she is beyond comfort and perhaps beyond help, but she has already announced her needs and the narrator begins to meet them. Although she complains and laments about many things in chapter 1, she asks for only one thing. She asks for God to see her: "YHWH, look at my affliction for the enemy has made himself great" (1:9c). Then she uses more emphatic language: "Look and pay attention for I have become worthless!" (1:11c).

When God does not respond she turns to the passersby (1:12a): "Is it nothing to you who pass by on the way? Look and pay attention!" They are silent as well, and she pleads with God again: "Look, YHWH, I am in anguish" (1:20a) and "Hear how I am groaning" (1:21a). What Daughter Zion wants desperately is a witness—someone who sees and hears the magnitude of her suffering.

The narrator comforts her because he alone sees her true suffering. His question "What can I say (*'ôd*) for you?" (2:13a) can be translated "How can I bear witness for you?" Although he seems to despair of comforting her, he offers the very things she seeks. He is her witness; he is her missing comforter. When he searches for a comparison for her pain and finds only the sea, vast, unfathomable, and uncontainable, he provides what she seeks. He sees her in the enormity of her pain and the life-flattening destruction that has befallen her. He apprehends the all-encompassing nature of her losses. His words mirror back her reality to her and validate her own perceptions of her pain. He acknowledges that her losses are as overwhelming as she experiences them to be, and the effect of his words is to provide her a companion in her pain.

The narrator no longer accuses Zion of bringing her tragedies upon herself; now he spreads the blame around. First, the prophets come under attack. Their task is to be mediators between God and the people and to lay before them visions of right covenant living, of proper relationship. Jeremiah also accuses the prophets of preaching falsely, of whitewashing the truth, and saying "peace, peace, when there is no peace" (Jer 6:14; 8:11). Some prophets lie to the people, offering their own messages instead of God's word (Jer 23:18-22).

According to the narrator, failure of religious leadership contributes to Zion's downfall. Twice he charges the prophets with seeing "empty and vain visions" (2:14a, c). In the middle of the same verse, he specifies the emptiness; the prophets' visions failed to show the city woman her own iniquity. Had they done so, she might have repented, changed her ways, turned toward God, and averted her present captivity. The failures leading to the city's destruction are not Zion's alone. The breakdown of truthfulness, fidelity, and true religious life pervades the community, and, for whatever reason, the prophets failed her.

The passersby fail her too (2:15). They offer neither help nor comfort, and they mock her and gloat disdainfully over her demise. The poet imagines their speech and quotes them as they pass by: "Is this the city that they say is 'the perfection of beauty, the joy of all the earth?'" The device of quoting the passersby who, in turn, quote others adds intensity to their mockery, already expressed by hissing and head shaking. Their description of her as the greatest beauty and the joy of all the earth is now so contrary to fact that they must ask if this is the same city woman.

The passersby may be cruel, but Zion's enemies deserve even greater blame (2:16). This verse, famously out of alphabetical order, also imagines the speech of others. The entire verse builds around the image of the enemies' mouths—"They opened their mouths" against her, "hissed, gnashed their teeth" and said, "We swallowed you up." The enemies' mouths are like maws that engulf, chew, and swallow the city. And like the passersby, they enact their joy with gestures and hissing. They are gleeful, exultant in their victory. They had longed for the day of triumph; now it has come and they have seen it. The contrast between what they see and what the narrator sees could not be more marked. They interpret her destruction as a glorious event; he sees a devastated and desolate city, like an abandoned and comfortless woman.

But the *'ayin* verse (2:17), in reverse alphabetical order from 2:16, brings the narrator's interpretation to a climax. The alphabetic reversal admits of many explanations among scholars, including speculations about simple scribal error or about the poem's origins in an early, unsettled stage of alphabetic development. But the reversal of letters may have literary significance. It draws our attention to the verses, and it mirrors the reversal of YHWH's former affection for Zion. "YHWH did what he planned. . . . He threw down and did not pity." Perhaps the "plans" the narrator means are other prophetic words against Judah that if Judah did not repent, it would be cast out of the land. Perhaps the plans refer to the assertions in Deuteronomy that life in the land depends upon fidelity and justice. But whatever lies behind God's plans, the verse implicates God in Zion's suffering above everyone else.

The alphabetic reversal in 2:16-17 places God's premeditated pitilessness at the climax of the narrator's interpretation. Zion's tragic suffering is now for him a tragedy caused by multiple failures, not by Zion's sin alone. The prophets defaulted, the passersby were indifferent, and the enemy greedily swallowed her up. But it was, above all, divine cruelty that "threw down," that "did not pity," that raised up the enemy. It is God's actions that have brought her to such a desperate place.

The previously disengaged narrator now becomes her passionate advocate. He uses a series of imperative verbs, commanding, urging, begging her to take action, to move from a passive and accepting victim of assault to an active and expressive agent of her own life. He addresses her directly, personifying the walls of the city to emphasize both her female and city identity. "Cry out with your heart to Adonai, O wall of Daughter Zion. Let tears run down like a torrent day and night. Do not let yourself stop; do not let your eyes be still" (2:18).

He does not intercede for her or speak for her. He speaks only to her and begs her to speak for herself, to call upon God with a barrage of tears, tears like torrential waters, tears that flow from running eyes that are never still (2:18). With these emotionally saturated urgings, the narrator may be trying to push the city woman out of the numbness that follows trauma. He may be begging her to plead on her own behalf because he has said such shocking things about God and cannot intercede for her. Or he may think that God will be moved by the city woman's tear-filled imprecations. He may realize that if she acts, she will be clinging to life by taking power in speech and gesture.

The Narrator Pleads for Action

The narrator reiterates his pleas. He tells the one who has been thrown down to "arise" (2:19a). She is to cause a scene, create a fuss, cry out in the night at the beginning of the watches, when guards come to take up the watch at the walls. She is to pour her heart out like water, as if her heart had become tears; she is to do this before the face of God. She is to stand before YHWH, encounter God, reveal her sobbing world to God, beg God, lift up her hands.

The narrator knows how to appeal to the city woman. She may not care enough to speak to God on her own behalf, but her heart is broken beyond repair over the suffering and loss of her children (2:19d). For their sake, she is to take action, to act up. Only God can heal her, comfort her, and intervene to save her children and her future. Perhaps if she who was once God's resting place, sanctuary, and chosen city went before the deity face to face, then God's unbridled and fierce rage might be withdrawn.

Look (2:20-22)

Res 2:20   Look, YHWH, and pay attention to whom you are acting so severely.

Should women eat their children, the children they have raised?[9]
Should priest and prophet be killed in the sanctuary of the Lord?

Sin 2:21   The young and the old lie down on the ground in the streets.
My virgins and my young men fall by the sword.
You killed them on the day of your anger; you slaughtered; you did not
  pity.

Taw 2:22   You summoned as on a feast day terrors all around.
And on the day of the anger of Yahweh no one escaped or survived.
Those whom I carried and reared, my enemy destroyed.

The narrator's attempt to arouse Daughter Zion to action works. She appeals directly to God, and is neither tactful nor indirect. She begins with her demand (2:20a), tells why she is making it, and then turns the petition back into a complaint. Her present demand is similar to previous ones (1:9c, 11c, 20a): "Look, YHWH, pay attention!" She uses the same Hebrew verbs *(rā'āh* and *nābaṭ),* the first meaning "to see," and the second "to see with attentiveness" or "to consider." Her demands imply that God has not been paying attention, not seeing her suffering, and if she could just get God to look carefully, God would stop afflicting her and would do something to help her. What she asks for explicitly, however, is simple and basic—only that God see her and the devastation and suffering of her children.

Zion's question underscores the hideous absurdity of her present world: "Should women eat their children?" (2:20b). Of course not! The situation is unthinkable, a violation of the human contract, of decency, and of covenant life. Women should not eat their offspring. Many interpretations of the mothers' cannibalism are possible. Women may actually have killed and eaten their children. If so, Zion's question reveals in a few words the profound destructiveness of the invasion upon the inhabitants of the city. Conversely, women may not be killing their children at all. Instead, Daughter Zion may be referring to the curse of Deuteronomy 28:53-57, warning Israel that infidelity to the covenant will result in cannibalism of children by both mothers and fathers. Daughter Zion may be using the deuteronomic curse to force YHWH to pay attention, to shock God into seeing that those curses have befallen the city. Even God must realize this is too much.

Whatever realities underlie Zion's question in the world created by this poetry, God must respond. How could God see these perversions and not cease from such evil? How can God know that priests and prophets are

---

[9] Hillers 34.

being killed in God's own sanctuary and not desist from this cruelty? Young and old, the priest and the prophet are lying in the streets, killed in the sanctuary, and destroyed by the sword.

Daughter Zion attempts to force God to take responsibility for the deaths: "You killed them on the day of your anger; you slaughtered; you did not pity" (2:21c). Again the human enemy is merely an agent of God, summoned as if to a feast day. Traditionally the day of YHWH referred to a future day when God would triumph over Israel's enemies. In this poem, however, the day has become a day of anger and catastrophe from which there is no escape. These are the realities that God must see. God may deny responsibility for her devastation, or may be inattentive and careless so as not fully to realize the consequences of anger and wild tantrums. Or the unthinkable may be true—YHWH may have deliberately inflicted these horrors upon her.

There is no response to Zion's petition. God does not speak. God does not comfort, restore health, return children, or bring life back to any semblance of order or of human dignity. In this poem, as in the previous one, God is silent. Daughter Zion is left with her tears, surrounded by devastation, alone without her children. She disappears as a literary figure in the book (except for 4:20) and only returns in the writing of the prophet known as Second Isaiah. But she has gained a witness, an advocate, and a companion in her suffering who sees, who pays attention, and who takes into consciousness the immeasurable, overwhelming power of her suffering. In the narrator Zion has found a comforter.

4

Mercies New Every Day

Lamentations 3

Occupying the center of five chapters, chapter 3 contains the only words of explicit hope in the book. Like a lull during a violent storm, poems of desolation and doubt surround it on both sides. The sudden appearance of hope in the middle of the book both startles and reassures, even as it creates one of the book's interpretive challenges. How is the hope of chapter 3 to be measured against the bleak poetic terrain around it? What is the nature of this hope, uttered as it is by someone who seems to be moving in and out of despair? Does the vivid hope of chapter 3 overpower the book's grim poetry to create "a theology of hope" (Gottwald 1954, 90-110)?

An anonymous new figure, whom I call "the strongman," is the chapter's principal speaker and the book's only articulator of hope. The poem refers to him as a *geber* (3:1, 35, 36, 39), that is, a male charged with the defense of "women, children, and other non-combatants" (Brown, Driver, and Briggs 150). But instead of defending others, the speaker himself is a captive, poignantly and shamefully unable to fulfill his protective role (Lanahan 45-46). His inability to defend even himself magnifies his powerlessness. In this poem the protector needs protection.

Provan (81) does not distinguish the voice of the strongman from that of the narrator in chapters 1 and 2, but the two speakers can hardly be the same. The narrator observes Zion's pain and never speaks of his own except in response to hers, but in chapter 3, the strongman's own suffering engulfs him. Tortured and spent, his laments are as heart-wrenching and pitiable as Zion's own. The strongman is a new poetic figure whose first-person account provides yet another picture of the catastrophe.

But the community also speaks in this poem, joining the strongman in corporate words of confession and lament (3:40-47), as if the people have been listening, and, at his invitation, step into the poetry.

Changes in Poetic Structures

This chapter ends in hopeful assurance, and changes in poetic structures from the two previous poems draw our attention to it. Like the first two chapters, chapter 3 also contains a sixty-six-line acrostic, but here the acrostic intensifies. Each of three consecutive verses begins with the same alphabetic letter. The poem's lines are shorter, it uses the *qinah* or limping meter more frequently, and Hebrew forms repeat and interweave more intricately across verses and stanzas. Finally, the expected cry of "how" (*'ēkāh*) is missing (1:1; 2:1; and see 4:1). These structural variations set the chapter apart from the other poems and suggest that it and its expressions of hope are the book's major focus. But that is not so.

Literary features of the last two chapters challenge and nearly overturn the strongman's hope. Chapters 4 and 5 emphatically reassert themes of doubt and despair, grow shorter, and in them the acrostic form diminishes and then disappears. The dour themes and structural diminutions of chapters 4 and 5 create a lopsided book. If they were of the same length as chapters 1 and 2, they would make a balanced frame around chapter 3 and the symmetry would clearly mark chapter 3 as the book's undisputed heart. But instead, these asymmetries disturb the seeming dominance of the strongman's voice and dump cold water on optimists seeking a quick escape from the book's painful world. Hope appears as an important interlude, a moment of calm in the storm, but merely one perspective among several in the aftermath of the invasion.

But even within this complex center poem, the strongman's hopeful testimony is fragile and uncertain. He vacillates so often between hope and despair that his hope remains ambiguous at best. This is not to deny the presence of hope in the poem but rather to question a long history of interpretation where hope washes away and silences the suffering and despair around it (Linafelt 2000, 17-18). It is not clear that hope is the book's radiant center nor that a theology of explicit hope dominates the book.

Instead, the realities of suffering and death and of a God remembered rather than encountered repeatedly moderate and overcome hope. Numerous times across the poem, the speaker flip-flops between doubt and hope in abrupt shifts typical of both the lament form and of healing processes. Hope rarely implants itself permanently or even enduringly after tragedy. Often survivors reenter their suffering, briefly see beyond it, and then fall back into pain and loss, only to emerge again much later.

Chapter 3 divides into two laments (3:1-42 and 3:43-66). This easy formal division led earlier interpreters to see the chapter as an amalgamation of previously existing poems, later unified by the acrostic form. The acrostic, however, is far too complex to have been imposed secondarily. The poem's repeated back-and-forth movement from complaint to hope, created by the double lament, expresses the poem's content and mimics the strongman's own flagging confidence as he struggles in his suffering.

The First Complaint

Trapped (3:1-21)

'Alep | 3:1 | I am the strongman who has seen affliction by the rod of his overflowing rage.

| 3:2 | He has led me and driven me into darkness, not light.

| 3:3 | Surely against me he has turned; he has turned his hand every day.

Bet | 3:4 | He has wasted my flesh and my skin; he broke my bones.

| 3:5 | He has built against me;[1] he has surrounded me with wormwood and weariness.

| 3:6 | He has set me in dark places like those long dead.

Gimmel | 3:7 | He has walled me in and I cannot escape; he has made my chain heavy.

| 3:8 | Even when I shout and cry for help, he shuts out my prayer.

| 3:9 | He has walled in my way with hewn stones; he has twisted my pathway.

Dalet | 3:10 | To me he is a bear lying in wait, a lion in secret places.

| 3:11 | He has turned aside my ways and torn me to pieces; he has made me desolate.

| 3:12 | He has bent his bow and set me up like a target for the arrow.

He | 3:13 | He has shot into my kidneys the arrows of his quiver.

| 3:14 | I have become the laughingstock to all my people,[2] their taunt song all the day.

| 3:15 | He has filled me with bitterness; he has saturated me with wormwood.

Waw | 3:16 | He has crushed my teeth with gravel; he has made me cower in the dust.

| 3:17 | My soul is rejected from peace; I have forgotten goodness.

| 3:18 | And I said, "My eminence has vanished and my hope from YHWH."

---

[1] For a different reading, see Fitzgerald 1967, 368-369; see also, Hillers 54.

[2] Some change *'ammî* to the plural, "all peoples." Provan (88) prefers the plural but such an emendation is unnecessary. See Albrektson 137.

Zayin   3:19 To remember[3] my affliction and my restless wandering is wormwood
             and gall.

          3:20 My soul remembers continually and sinks[4] down upon me.

          3:21 (But) this I call to mind; therefore, I hope.

The strongman relates his experience of captivity in first-person speech. Like Daughter Zion, he claims the authority of a survivor and testifies to pain from within the experience. "I am the strongman who has seen *(rā'āh)* affliction *('ŏnî)* by the rod of his overflowing rage" (3:1). His experience of affliction—the Hebrew word "to see" also means "to experience"—embodies the community's massive suffering. The enemy encircles and entraps him (Lanahan 46), and his first-person testimony invites us to relive his suffocating captivity with him.

The strongman's first complaint intertwines causes of his suffering with descriptions of it (3:1-19). Although he is the grammatical subject of the first verse, through most of the complaint he is the direct object (3:1-19). An assailant attacks him violently, but he withholds the assailant's identity (3:2-16, except for verse 14). By leaving the enemy unnamed, he provokes curiosity, heightens tension, and leads readers into the tangled relationship between torturer and victim. His frequent use of first-person and third-person pronouns (I and he) suggests an intimacy between himself and his opponent and makes all the more dramatic the unspeakable betrayal that becomes evident only later in the poem.

The strongman's complaints are claustrophobic. His enemy drives him into darkness, turns against him, and turns "his hand every day" (3:3). The attacks are daily and physical as the enemy wastes his flesh and breaks his bones, as if the strongman were an animal being slaughtered for a meal (3:4). His enemy builds against him, surrounds him with wormwood and weariness, and erects a hut or a prison, a dark place cut off from life, a place forgotten where no one can reach him, "like those long dead" (3:6).

Prison building continues in the third stanza (3:7-9). In the same way that the enemy encircles and "walls in" the strongman, so the stanza imprisons his cries for help, and his prayer (3:8). The repetition of the verb "to wall in" *(gādar*, 3:7, 9) erects verbal walls around his pleas (3:8). The enemy walled him in; his chain is heavy (3:7). The walls are impenetrable, made of hewn stone; his pathway forward is twisted (3:9). How can his

---

   [3] *Zĕkār* may be an imperative or an infinitive construct. The LXX reads "I remember," but the infinitive makes more sense in view of verse 20 which seems to continue the thought of verse 19.

   [4] Reading *šwḥ* ("to be bowed down," Provan 91) and making *napšî* ("my soul") the verse's subject with the LXX.

cries and prayers for help escape from such a solid prison? (3:8). His enemy traps him, chains him, and silences him. It is not enough that walls surround him; they also snuff out his cries and prayers.

Because he cannot gain a witness to his suffering, his captivity dehumanizes him further. He cannot bring his pain to speech. His words cannot reach outside his prison for help, human or divine. Like Daughter Zion, he needs a recipient of his anguish, but the prospect is hopeless and he is isolated in his affliction.

The strongman's imagery shifts from entrapment and imprisonment to violent assault, first by an animal-like enemy and then by a military enemy (3:10-16). Because attacks follow imprisonment, the poetry implies that the enemy corners the strongman in prison and then attacks him at his most vulnerable and defenseless, when he has no hope of escape. He is helpless, walled in by hewn stones. His attacker is a "bear lying in wait" and "a lion in secret places." The attack is sudden and unexpected, perpetrated by a ferocious beast that tears him "to pieces" and leaves him "desolate" (3:10-11).

His imagery for the attacker shifts from beasts to a warrior with bow and arrows whose target is the strongman. The archer shoots an arrow into the strongman's innards (3:13), and he becomes a "laughingstock" (3:14), an object of shame before the people he is supposed to protect. Now they taunt him. The nameless one who imprisoned and attacked him has filled him with bitterness, saturated him with poisonous and bitter-tasting wormwood (3:15, echoing 3:5 and anticipating 3:19).

The enemy's attacks spill into the next stanza: "He has crushed my teeth with gravel," and "made me cower in the dust" (3:16). Perhaps the strongman is rummaging in the grass for food (Renkema 73), or perhaps his enemy tortures him by forcing gravel between his teeth. Whatever the phrase means, the strongman's predicament is exceedingly painful and dehumanizing. But suddenly, in reflecting on his spiritual condition within his prison, the strongman again becomes the acting subject of the poetry: "My soul is rejected from peace; I have forgotten goodness" (3:17). How could it be otherwise? How could he remember "good" in the midst of overpowering dehumanization? Then he quotes himself. "I said, 'My eminence has vanished and my hope from YHWH'" (3:18).

His hopeless thoughts about his affliction run over into the next stanza (3:19-21) and with verse 1, enclose his precise afflictions (3:2-18) in a verbal frame (3:1 and 19). The very act of remembering his affliction and his wandering is "wormwood and gall" (3:19). Like most who have suffered profoundly and totally, his soul "sinks down" upon him (3:20). He cannot forget his trauma; it is ever alive within, needing to be told and retold, like a weight pressing upon him and crushing him.

The strongman's first-person account of his affliction (3:1-19) is not exact in any narrative sense, but it is an accurate and effective depiction of horror. All the more startling, then, is the final verse of this section. In the first of many reversals of outlook, he thinks of something that changes everything: "This I call to mind; therefore, I hope" (3:21). By changing his mind in the midst of a stanza, he weaves hope and despair together in shocking abruptness. Although mood shifts are typical of lament forms in which speakers often move quickly from complaint to assurance and praise, the strongman moves back and forth so frequently that he appears to wobble in uncertainty. His hopefulness never fully yields to praise.

Divine Mercies

The section (3:22-42) subdivides into three parts: Reasons to Hope (3:22-36), The Dilemma (3:37-39), and A Call to Repent (3:40-42).

Reasons to Hope (3:22-36)

Het 3:22 The steadfast love of YHWH is not finished,[5] for his mercies do not come to an end.

3:23 (They are) new every morning. Great is your faithfulness.

3:24 "YHWH is my portion," says my soul; therefore, I hope in him.

Tet 3:25 Good is YHWH to those who wait for him and to the soul who seeks him.

3:26 Good it is to wait without stirring[6] for the salvation of YHWH.

3:27 Good it is for the strongman that he bears the yoke in his youth,

Yod 3:28 That he sits alone and is silent when he lays it upon him,

3:29 That he puts his mouth in the dust; perhaps there is still hope,

3:30 That he gives his cheek to the smiter; he is filled with insult.

Kap 3:31 For Adonai does not reject forever.[7]

3:32 For he causes grief, but he has mercy according to the greatness of his steadfast love.

3:33 For he does not afflict willingly nor grieve the children of humans.

---

[5] Reading *tammū* (Hillers 56; and Westermann 1994, 140).

[6] For this translation, see Levine.

[7] This verse is short and has led to unnecessary efforts to lengthen it, but its shortness emphasizes it (Renkema 405).

Lamed   3:34 To crush[8] under his feet all prisoners of war,
         3:35 To turn aside the case of the strongman before the face of the Most
               High,
         3:36 To subvert a human in his cause, Adonai does not see.

What the strongman "calls to mind" (3:21) could not be more surprising in view of the suffering he has just related (3:1-20). In an extraordinary statement of faith, he remembers that YHWH's love is not over, not "finished"; YHWH's mercies never end, "they are new every morning" (3:22-23). Then, for the first time in the poem, he addresses God directly, as though God had been his silent audience all along and he knows he can turn and make contact with the divine Eavesdropper. "Great is your faithfulness!" he proclaims. To emphasize his point, he quotes himself again: "'YHWH is my portion,' says my soul; therefore, I hope in him" (3:23-24).

The taproot of the strongman's hope, the unseen source of his confidence, is God's own faithful character, affirmed in many places in the Old Testament (Fretheim 25). In the abundant plural, God never stops showing mercies and loving-kindness. Every morning God's newborn mercies surprise and overturn. Though the strongman's life is in ruins and trauma encompasses his being, in his own deep act of faithfulness, he remembers that YHWH is his "portion." God's faithfulness is his possession, his "habitual mode of life," his chosen way of living (Brown, Driver, and Briggs 324).

The poem could stop here. This passionate outpouring could be the end of the strongman's words, his complaint resolved in trust and hope. But the strongman's suffering is too deep to be overturned for long by simple theological affirmation. In the next three stanzas (3:25-36), he tells himself and his readers why it is good to wait for salvation. Perhaps he is trying to convince himself and his audience that hope is reliable and appropriate despite evidence to the contrary.

The next four stanzas (3:25-36) explain further why hope is suitable, though how the verses fit together is uncertain and doubt shadows that hope (Dobbs-Allsopp 1997, 48; Provan 22). "Good is YHWH" to the one who waits and seeks. "Good it is to wait without stirring," without breathing, fixed in place, for the "salvation of YHWH." Good it is for the strongman *(geber)* to "bear the yoke in his youth." Good, good, good it is for the burdened and enslaved to wait, to anticipate, to long for, to be ready when God will save. The waiting ones are special to God, claims the strongman. The

---

[8] The infinitive constructs of verses 34-36 provide *lamed*s for the acrostic but pose syntactical problems. The question is whether these clauses provide examples of the affliction and grief that God does not willingly cause (verse 33, Hillers 58), or exemplify what Adonai does not see in verse 36 (Westermann 1994, 38).

three repetitions of the word "good" create the impression that goodness requires repetition to become convincing, particularly since this is only one of two stanzas that repeat a word at the beginning of three lines.

The next stanza expands the strongman's instructions to himself with spiritual disciplines for an imprisoned man to practice (3:28-30). He should sit alone and be silent under his burden, put his mouth in the dust, and give his cheek to the one who smites. But the disconcerting result of this advice is that it undermines the hope enjoined earlier. "Perhaps there is still hope" (3:29) means that hope is fragile, unstable, perhaps even nonexistent. The strongman's hope falters.

Quickly he piles on more reasons to hope and to be submissive (3:31-36), but simultaneously he implicates God in his suffering. "Adonai does not reject forever" (3:31), he proclaims. The power of this verse stretches backward and forward in the poem. It occurs in the stanza at the alphabetic midpoint of the acrostic, is noticeably shorter than any other line in the poem, and begins the second of only two stanzas that repeat the opening word (3:31-33). All these features draw attention to the verse and make it distinctive in the poem. Unequivocally, it interprets the speaker's plight as the result of divine rejection.

The theological dilemma implicit in the strongman's complaint (3:1-20) becomes clear in this short, punching line. God rejects, but not forever (3:31). God causes grief but possesses mercy immeasurable (3:32). Herein lies the theological tension residing at the poem's heart. The remainder of the poem struggles with the conflict between divine rejection and divine mercy.

Then the strongman tries to defend God who "does not afflict willingly nor grieve the children of humans" (3:33). God does not do these things "willingly" (literally "from his heart," *millibbô*). In Hebrew, the heart is the symbol of decision and will, not of feeling, as in modern English. Here the strongman asserts that the Divine Punisher—the source of his affliction (3:1-19)—is acting against the divine will. Instead of willingly aggrieving and afflicting, he implies, God may be powerless over affliction or, at least, internally conflicted about it. Perhaps chaotic forces outside divine control or forces set in action by human sinfulness corner God into punishing the sinful. Or perhaps the Creator has chosen to become vulnerable to the world and its people, so that God does not "afflict willingly" (3:33).

The next verses (3:34-36) add grammatical ambiguity and increase theological uncertainty. Infinitive verbs in each verse may extend the thought of the previous line and specify afflictions that God does not willingly cause: to crush prisoners, to turn aside the legal cause of the strongman *(geber)*, and to subvert a human in his legal case or covenant lawsuit (Hillers 58). Or instead, the infinitives might belong with the last clause of the stanza and simply name actions that "Adonai does not see" (*rā'āh*, 3:36a). If God did see the crushing of prisoners and legal injustices, then perhaps God would act. But the God of Lamentations is a blind God who, when asked to look, see, or pay attention (1:9, 11, 20; 2:20), does not respond.

Rather than needing resolution, the stanza's grammatical ambiguities may express the strongman's theological confusion. He cannot resolve the contradiction between his confidence in God (3:21-33) and torture and abuse he has experienced (3:1-20), nor can his audience, whose suffering he embodies. He brings his dilemma into the open in the next stanza with three rhetorical questions.

The Dilemma (3:37-39)

Mem   3:37   Who can speak and it happens, if Adonai does not command?

            3:38   Do not the good and the bad both go out from the mouth of the Most High?

            3:39   What living human will complain, what strongman, about his sin?

When tragedy occurred, the ancients believed God caused it, and this assumption lies at the heart of the speaker's struggle. Is not God's word all-powerful? Does not everything come from God's mouth? What strongman (*geber*) can "complain about his sin?" The third question jumps to the conclusion that humans cause their own suffering by their sins and therefore have no cause to complain (3:39, Provan 99; but see Gordis 1974b, 183-184). But if the strongman is indirectly chiding complainers in his community, then he has forgotten his own lengthy complaint at the poem's beginning (3:1-19), or he rethinks it and concludes that no one has a right to complain, since human sin forces God to act.

Hidden behind his questions is a long theological tradition. Deuteronomy and the prophets taught that Israel's life in the land and its identity as a covenanted people hinged upon their obedience to God's word. Disobedience would bring destruction and exile from the land. The strongman's questions set this traditional view before his audience, as if he is seeking agreement and support for it. By blaming human sinfulness for the catastrophe, he justifies God's deeds and this leads him to confession.

A Call to Repent (3:40-42)

Nun   3:40   Let us test and examine thoroughly our ways, and let us turn to YHWH.

            3:41   Let us lift up our hearts (along) with our hands to El in the heavens.

            3:42   We have transgressed and rebelled; you have not forgiven!

Now the strongman invites the entire community to confess its sin in the hope that confession will bring about a new reality. As if the people have been following him all along, he draws them into the poem and urges them to examine their ways, turn to God, lift up hearts and hands in public gestures, and declare their sinfulness (3:40-42a). But about that sinfulness, he says little. Instead, he speaks of a general sinful condition in conventional abstract terms. "We have transgressed and rebelled." He names no specific offenses like abandoning God, living unjustly, or worshiping idols in a perfunctory and conventional confession.

But abruptly he and the community change direction in another turn away from hope. "We have transgressed and rebelled; you have not forgiven!" (3:42). We did our part, he implies; we have turned to you, we have confessed our sins, but you have let us down. You have not reciprocated, turned to us, or forgiven us. The community alone cannot be the cause of this suffering; God, too, is implicated.

The Strongman's Second Complaint

The strongman's attack on God leads into the second section of the chapter (3:42b-66). There a new complaint echoes language of the first complaint (3:1-42a, cf. 3:1-19; cf. 3:1 and 43; 3:8 and 44; 3:4, 7-9 and 47-48, 53; and 3:10, 52). But the second complaint is broader, more expansive, and more direct. In both intensified bitterness and brighter confidence, the second complaint probes the nation's suffering with deeper questions and cancels any reconciling potential of the communal confession. Hope disappears and reappears again. The second complaint divides into three sections: Sunk in a Pit (3:43-54), God Has Seen (3:55-63), and Plea for Justice (3:64-66).

Sunk in a Pit (3:43-54)

Samek   3:43   You have covered us with anger and pursued us; you have killed and you have not pitied.

         3:44   You have covered yourself with a cloud so that prayers cannot pass through.

         3:45   Scum and refuse you have made us in the midst of the peoples.

Pe   3:46   They opened their mouths against us—all our enemies.

         3:47   Dread and a pit have come to us, devastation and breaking.

         3:48   Rivers of tears run down from my eyes over the breaking of the daughter of my people.

'Ayin   3:49   My eyes pour out without stopping and there is no end,

         3:50   Until YHWH looks down from heaven and sees.

         3:51   My eyes act perversely against me because of all the daughters of my city.

Sade   3:52 My enemies hunted me like a bird without cause.

3:53 In the pit they put an end to my life; they threw a stone over me.

3:54 Waters flowed over my head. I said, "I am cut off!"

The strongman's angry accusations against God contrast sharply with his earlier call for repentance. God has failed them, God is unfaithful, and God's very character is in question as God covers up and covers over (3:43, 44). God's first covering up is an act of aggression against them. God covers them with anger, pursues them, and kills them without pity. The human military invader completely coalesces with God in this accusation and makes the earlier communal repentance appear ritualistic and halfhearted.

In the second covering-up God protects God's self from the people, reversing the usual divine-human relationship. "You have covered yourself with a cloud so that prayers cannot pass through" (3:44). Ephemeral but unbreachable, the cloud cover forms an impenetrable barrier against the people's prayers. The cloud-covered God is invisible, hidden, and beyond reach. Their relationship has come to an impasse of God's own making. And besides absconding from their world, God has made them "scum and refuse" among the peoples (3:45).

Without confidence in God, there is only dread and panic in the spiritually empty world. The strongman shifts attention from God's absence to the presence of human enemies—they have spoken "against us" (3:46). In Hebrew, euphonically related nouns fall on either side of the verb and direct object. Sound effects are lost in English, but the heavy burden of destruction is still evident. "Dread *(pahad)* and a pit *(pahat)* have come to us, devastation *(haššē't)* and breaking *(haššaber)*" (3:47). Although the phrasing is awkward in English ("a pit coming to us"), Hebrew sounds amplify the suffering. Dread, an overwhelming fear of the future, governs them in a pit of doubt and hopelessness. The strongman weeps a river of tears over the "breaking of the daughter of my people" (3:48). The "shattering" of Jerusalem, again personified as a woman, provokes his tears, as he begins to sound like the narrator in chapter 2.

The strongman's tears flow without end in two stanzas, again in reverse alphabetical order (3:49-51 and 3:52-54). Reasons for the alphabetic inversion are not clear, but it has the effect of drawing our attention to the verses just as the narrator demands that God must see. Eyes blurred by tears (3:49 and 51) frame God's seeing that alone would staunch those tears (3:50). The strongman's tears, which he calls eyes acting "perversely," are a passionate response to suffering and an insistent political posture before God. The strongman will weep endlessly to persuade, to demand, and to force God's attention, "Until YHWH looks down from heaven and sees" *(rā'āh,*

3:50). Like Zion, the strongman has only one need, one request that will bring an end to his sorrow. God must look down from the hiding place in the clouds and "see" the full reality of the breaking and shattering of the city. For anything to change, God must see. He will weep until then.

In a stanza that marks a nadir of hopelessness and has caused many interpreters to associate the speaker with Jeremiah, the strongman returns to his own predicament (3:52-54). Though earlier in the poem he insisted suffering was punishment for sin (3:39), now he claims that the enemies' attacks are unprovoked, "without cause" (3:52). He is innocent of anything that would bring this suffering upon him. His enemies hunt him like a bird, put him in a pit, cut off his life, and put a stone over him (see Jer 38:1-6). As waters flow over his head, he quotes himself, "I am cut off!" (3:54). Few more claustrophobic, dehumanizing tortures are imaginable; death hovers over the waters as they rise to engulf him.

It is not clear whether the events in the pit depict the speaker's physical experience, or his emotional and spiritual collapse, or both. What is clear is that the strongman has reached the bottom of possibility. He has come to an impasse beyond which he cannot see and out of which he cannot escape. "I am cut off!" (3:54) means not only that light and air are shut off and he is isolated from the human community, but that the future itself has vanished. Not surprisingly, at the bottom of the pit, when all is lost, the strongman changes his outlook yet again.

God Has Seen (3:55-63)

Qop   3:55 I called your name, YHWH, from the bottom of the pit.

         3:56 You have heard my voice; do not hide your ears from my breathing and my cry for help.

         3:57 You have drawn near on the day I called you and you have said, "Do not fear."

Res   3:58 Adonai, you have pleaded the cause of my soul; you have redeemed my life.

         3:59 YHWH, you have seen my deprivation of justice; judge my cause.

         3:60 You have seen all their vengeance, all their plots against me.

Sin   3:61 You have heard their insults, all their plots against me.

         3:62 The lips of the ones rising and their imaginings are against me all the day.

         3:63 Pay attention to their sitting and their rising. I am their taunt song.

Inexplicably, from the pit the strongman bursts out in prayers of hope, the nature of which is not clear. He may be remembering a past experience of rescue (Hillers 15, 52-53, 59; Gordis 1974b, 186-187; Gottlieb 57-60; Provan 106); his pleas for God "to see" may imagine rescue already accomplished in hope, if not in fact (Provan 108); or he may be voicing his inherited tradition of hope (Fretheim 130). The strongman's enemies hunt him (3:52), put him in a pit, and close him in with a stone (3:53). He is drowning, cut off from life (3:54). From that place of hopelessness and dread, he addresses YHWH directly. "I called your name" (3:55).

Tensions and contradictions mark the strongman's hope in the next stanzas (3:56-61). He continues to use perfect verbs (completed action) to express confidence, or perhaps wishful thinking, that deliverance is at hand, as if calling on God were enough to effect a different future. "You have heard my voice; do not hide your ears" (3:56). He believes God has heard him, yet he fears rejection and abandonment. On the day I called you said, "Do not fear" (3:57). These reassuring words are the only words attributed to God in the book, but they are not direct speech; they are either remembered conversation from the past or a traditional affirmation the strongman remembers.

In confident hope or distant remembering, the strongman reminds God, "You have pleaded the cause of my soul" (3:58). He already said that God would not turn away his "case" (3:35-36); now he claims that YHWH has seen (*rā'āh*; 3:59, 60) the vengeance and plots against him. He begs God to act as judge against his enemies, and he forgets completely about his own calls for repentance earlier in the chapter. This suffering arises from unjust enemies, not from the sins of the community. Now he proclaims that God has seen the treachery, the insults, and taunting songs of the enemies (3:61-63). Perhaps the enemies' injustice will provoke God to action, even if his own plight does not stir God to pity.

Like Daughter Zion in the previous chapters (1:11, 20; 2:20), the strongman demands that God "pay attention" (*nābaṭ*, 3:63). If only God would really look, really "observe with penetrating care" (Renkema 463), perhaps a new future—any future at all—would be possible.

Plea for Justice

Taw 3:64 Return recompense to them, YHWH, according to the work of their hands.

3:65 Give them obstinacy[9] of heart; your curse be upon them.

3:66 Pursue them in anger and exterminate them from under the heavens of YHWH.

Still addressing YHWH directly, the strongman begs for vengeance. His requests are violent; he wants the enemy to be in his shoes. Repay them for

---

[9] The meaning of the word is unclear; its literal sense is "covering."

"the work of their hands"; make their hearts obstinate; curse them; pursue them; exterminate them. Do all this in anger. Since the strongman experienced God's overflowing rage, he wants as much for his enemies. He wants to balance the scales, restore justice, have his enemies know what he has known. He does not retaliate himself or suggest that others do. Instead, he begs God to bring about justice.

Inexplicable Hope

Like other speakers in the book, the strongman is an individual whose plight signifies aspects of the community's suffering (Renkema 344). Trapped, tortured, and despairing, he leads us with him to the place of vanished hope— "I am lost!" He invites us to follow his lead: to wait, be silent, stop complaining, and urges us to abase ourselves, to repent, and to turn wholeheartedly to YHWH. He plunges us into his theological dilemma concerning God's role in their suffering—"Do not the good and the bad both go out from the mouth of the Most High?" (3:38).

The strongman never resolves his intellectual dilemma—that God causes both good and bad. Yet when he reaches his lowest moment at the bottom of the pit, he inexplicably finds hope. The impulse toward hope occurs in him, not in his circumstances, which have not changed. He remembers past assurances or has new experience of God's presence, and he becomes confident that God "has seen" the enemies' oppression and will take action against them.

The poem's contradictions leave it theologically conflicted, but biblical hope does not emerge from proper reasoning or new information. It is not optimism or wishful thinking. It is not a simple act of the will, a decision under human control, or a willful determination. It emerges without clear cause like grace, without explanation, in the midst of despair and at the point of least hope. It comes from elsewhere, unbidden, illusive, uncontrollable, and surprising, given in the pit, the place of no hope.

The strongman's hope is unsteady; it comes, goes, and comes again repeatedly. It is not Lamentations' overriding and triumphant interpretation of the tragedy, for the grief and despair in the following chapters quickly subdue it. But by decentering the book's hope, I do not mean to eradicate it. I recognize, instead, that hope is one experience of survival, one interlude in coming to grips with tragedy, and one fragile interpretation among others. Hope appears, flags, disappears as if forever, reemerges, and fades again as the light changes.

5

Beaten Down

Lamentations 4

After the strongman's intense anger, pain, and hope, chapter 4 is a massive letdown. Its two speakers, an unidentified narrator and the people, appear exhausted and hopeless. Everything about the poem—its tone, structures, and even its length—diminishes, grows smaller and less intense, even though the scenes are as vividly horrifying as anything in the book so far. Chapter 4, or at least the first sixteen verses spoken by an unnamed narrator, seem to be uttered in a monotone, as if the tragedy has left him stunned and depleted.

Shrinking

The poem expresses diminishment, a shriveling of feelings, a closing of horizons. Even its poetic structures convey exhaustion. Rather than continuing the intensified acrostic of chapter 3, chapter 4 returns to the acrostic style of chapters 1 and 2, but even that is abbreviated. Like the first two chapters, chapter 4 begins with the "How" *('ēkāh)* of the funeral dirge, and it, too, restricts its acrostic to the first word of each stanza. The stanzas, however, contain only two lines rather than three, making a short forty-four line poem rather than the sixty-six-line poems of each of the first three chapters. The shortened form signals the content, a famine of food and of hope.

With short, clipped vignettes, the narrator takes us on a tour of the city after the invasion. He directs our gaze to the desolate conditions facing survivors, conjuring up brutal scenes of mothers and children and of the effects of hunger on old and young. By alternating his attention between domestic and public scenes, he shows that the invasion destroyed every aspect of communal life. In the foreground of his tour through the city is the tragic fate of the children.

The poem's principal speaker resembles the narrator in chapter 1. He is anonymous, and his tone is observational and uninvolved. But even if he is the same figure, his characterization is not the point in this chapter. He never uses first-person speech, nor are his words supplemented by the more intense, personal testimony of either Daughter Zion or the strongman. Rather, his words sweep across the destruction, letting it speak for itself in its depravity and deprivation.

The poem's second speaker is the people (4:17-22). It is their plural voice that provides dramatic, first-person testimony about the invasion itself, spoken of here directly for the first time in the book. But in a significant departure from previous chapters, neither the narrator nor the people ever speak to or demand anything of God. Perhaps they are completely hopeless that God will ever see, act, or save, or perhaps this chapter serves as an introduction to the long petition of chapter 5, in which the people continue to speak. Yet the acrostic form sets this chapter apart from the next one, so that together the two poems simultaneously pull toward and away from one another in a swirling contradiction of forces (Grossberg 83-104).

The shortened acrostic, less personal voice, and absence of address to God convey obliquely what the poem's content presents explicitly. The survivors' strength, emotional responsiveness, and capacity to reach for help have shrunk and grown dim like the city's gold (4:1). Resignation and despair have triumphed over anger and resistance. Life recedes and slips away with the ephemeral hope of the previous chapter.

The poem divides into four thematic units: Everything Grows Dim (4:1-10), Why This Has Happened (4:11-16), Retelling the Invasion (4:17-20), and Future Reversals (4:21-22).

The narrator speaks in the poem's first two units (4:1-10, 11-16). This narrator is a disembodied voice, a tired witness, giving us a glimpse of fading life.

Everything Grows Dim (4:1-10)

'Alep 4:1   How the gold has become dim, how the pure gold has changed,
          Scattered like the sacred stones at the head of every street.

Bet 4:2   The precious children of Zion, who were weighed as pure gold,
          How they are accounted like an earthen jar, the mere work of a potter's hands.

Gimmel 4:3 Even jackals offer the breast and nurse their young,[1]
But the daughter" of my people is cruel like ostriches in the wilderness.

Dalet 4:4 The tongue of the infant sticks to the roof of its mouth in thirst.
Children ask for food, but no one spreads out food before them.

He 4:5 Those who ate delicious things perish in the streets.
Those who were raised in purple clothing now embrace ash heaps.[2]

Waw 4:6 And greater is the iniquity[3] of the daughter of my people than the sins of Sodom.
The overturning was as in a moment though no hands were raised against her.

Zayin 4:7 Her princes were shining as snow; they dazzled like milk.
Their bodies were ruddy, their forms like sapphire.

Het 4:8 Their forms are darker than soot; they are not recognized in the streets.
Their skin has shriveled upon their bones; they are dried up like a tree.

Tet 4:9 Better off those pierced by the sword than those pierced by hunger,
Than those who waste away, pierced by (no) produce from the field.[4]

Yod 4:10 The hands of merciful women boiled their children.
They became food for them in the breaking of the daughter of my people.

The narrator tours the streets and finds there the children whose suffering and death frame the verses and embody the tragedy of the nation (4:2-4, 10). If there are no children, the people's extinction is at hand. The children's suffering gives poignant anguish to the narrator's words, but despite their shocking condition, the narrator understates the fractures of communal life that have worn down everyone.

Another dirge announces the death of the city yet again, but in a puzzling and suggestive manner. "How (*'ēkāh*) the gold has become dim, how (*'ēkāh*) the pure gold has changed" (4:1). Pure gold has changed in some way, but

---

[1] Correcting to *tanîm*.
[2] See Renkema 507.
[3] *'Awon* can mean "iniquity" or "punishment." Either Zion's sins were greater or her punishment was swifter than Sodom's.
[4] Renkema (5-16) argues that emendation of the text is unnecessary if *dābaq* is taken figuratively. The Hebrew is difficult and uncertain (Hillers 81).

as Hillers (78-79) notes, pure gold does not tarnish, darken, or grow dim. For gold to tarnish means the inconceivable has happened—pure gold has dimmed and "scattered like the sacred stones at the head of every street" (4:1). The darkening and careless scattering of the gold signifies the dimming and tarnishing of life. That its reference is not clear adds to the poetic possibilities.

Gold may refer to the permanent beauty of the city, now tarnished and destroyed like the temple and its scattered stones; ruins of the once "golden" city litter the streets. Or the dulled gold may evoke the children's dimmed future. The lives of the "precious children of Zion, who were weighed as pure gold" (using yet a third synonym for gold), are tarnished and scattered about (4:2). Precious children, once reckoned like pure gold, the community's glittering, shining wealth, its future security, are now as worthless pottery, no more valuable than a cheap jar, easily broken and disposable. How the gold has grown dim.

Images of the cruelty of Mother Zion and of the city mothers toward their children overlap (4:2-3). Zion's children have become worthless, and Zion treats them with even less care than the most despised animals show their offspring. Even jackals nurse their children, but Zion is as cruel as ostriches who are notorious for neglect of their young (see Job 39:13-16). The city's mothers repeat Zion's mistreatment of her children against their own children. Dying of hunger and thirst, the children ask for food, but no one gives them anything to eat (4:4). City woman Zion becomes a figure of cruelty in this poem rather than of pity, as she was in the first two chapters. She portrays the utter dehumanization of survivors, reduced to vicious behavior against their own children in the obscene effects of the invasion upon communal and domestic life.

The poem does not report whether parents withhold food and drink because of famine or viciousness. Indeed, the terse, economical description creates a world of imagination made more horrible by its sparseness. The narrator tells nothing of the mothers' suffering, only laying out the tragedy of the children, sharp as sketches engraved on stone. Children are starving, and their lives fade away. Mothers live in excruciating pain as their breasts dry up and food supplies disappear.

Food links the fate of the children in the streets to the fate of people at the other end of the social scale. Royalty, who once wore purple and ate delicious foods, now dwell on ash heaps (4:5). Those whom once comfort, honor, and wealth embraced, now themselves embrace degradation upon ash heaps. The nobility's change of circumstance could not be more striking. In a democracy of deprivation, the city's destruction affects everyone, and even the most advantaged and the most protected are brought low. The narrator briefly interrupts himself to comment on the cause (4:6); the city's iniquity surpasses that of mythic Sodom (Gen 19).

Contrasts between the present and past of the upper classes reveal the extent of the invasion's destructiveness (4:7-8). Wealthy young princes pass by in the streets, and no one can recognize them. Once their bodies glowed with ruddy health, like snow or milk; their forms were strong and sharply etched like precious sapphire. But good health and physical beauty have fled as their bodies bear the imprint of their suffering. They look burned up like soot; their skin is shriveled dry as wood, and no one recognizes them in the streets for their faces are altered beyond the people's remembrance of them.

Conditions are so appalling that the narrator remarks quietly in the style of a wisdom saying—"Better off those pierced by the sword" (4:9). Those "pierced by the sword" die quickly, but survivors "pierced by hunger" meet death in a slow, suffocating embrace.

Mercy Destroyed

Despair takes on a life of its own as the narrator returns to the domestic space occupied by mothers and children. There the expected bond between mother and child has dissolved in horror beyond words—"The hands of merciful women boiled their children" (4:10). We can hardly imagine a more depraved condition of the populace as a most basic human bond is ripped to pieces and mothers cook the bodies of their own children. And these are the *raḥămānîyôt*, the compassionate, merciful mothers. The word for merciful comes from the same Hebrew root the strongman uses to speak of God's mercies, "new every morning" (3:23). The merciful nature of the mothers turned to cannibalism of their own children adds one more detail of communal abasement in the destroyed society.

The poem echoes Daughter Zion's desperate plea to God in chapter 2: "Should women eat their children, the children they have raised?" (2:20). Domestic space—safe, secure, and nurturing—has become a site of depravity. Mercies are a mockery, and the society implodes upon itself in violence turned inward. How could this happen when children were immensely important to mothers, not only through bonds of affection but also because children gave them status and protection in old age? How could mothers destroy their own future?

Several explanations of these verses are possible. If women did participate in cannibalism, it may have been to feed other starving children. Mothers may have boiled bodies of dead children to feed those surviving. Or it may not be literal, but rather a symbolic fulfillment of a curse in Deuteronomy that described what would happen if Israel violated its covenant with God.

> In the desperate straits to which the enemy siege reduces you, you will eat the fruit of your womb, the flesh of your sons and daughters whom the LORD your God has given you. Even the most refined and gentle of men among you will begrudge food to his own brother, to the wife whom he embraces, and to the last of his remaining children, giving to none of them any of the flesh of his children whom he is eating, because nothing else remains to him, in the desperate straits to which the enemy siege will reduce you in all your towns. She who is the most refined and gentle among you, so gentle and refined that she does not venture to set the sole of her foot on the ground, will begrudge food to the husband whom she embraces, to her own son, and to her own daughter, begrudging even the afterbirth that comes out between her thighs, and the children that she bears, because she is eating them in secret for lack of anything else, in the desperate straits to which the enemy siege will reduce you in your towns. (Deut 28:53-57, NRSV)

In Lamentations, the narrator reports the fulfillment of this curse but omits references to the fathers' cruelty and desperation. The narrator levels charges only at mothers. This focus on mothers may be a poetic decision that sets images of mothers and children within the larger image of Mother Zion and her children. It may suggest that men are not around in the invasion's aftermath, or it may scapegoat women in a desire to protect men from such hideous accusations. Or it may be a literary detail chosen precisely for its horrifying nature as it depicts a world turned upside-down in a swirling chaos of dehumanization and brutality. This is what the enemy has wrought against a whole people.

The poetry simply does not offer enough evidence to decide about its nuances, nor does it comment on the suffering of mothers and children. Whatever the significance of the cannibalism in this poem, it reveals the devastation of a people whose children cannot survive and whose mothers invert their normal role of nurture and protection. Claudia Camp (108), writing about two cannibalizing women in 2 Kings 6:24-33, notes, "Indeed, a mother whose maternal instinct has failed symbolizes a world in chaos." Gina Hens-Piazza adds that "the women's story becomes a ledger upon which the moral status of the community is assessed." Do they represent moral decay as society's accomplices or victims? These questions aimed at another text illuminate this one as well. There is no future for this people (O'Connor 1998b, 190).

Why This Has Happened (4:11-16)

The second part of the narrator's speech continues his tour of the streets, and he shifts blame from Zion and the mothers to community leaders. They have committed shocking, bloody crimes and public failures.

Kap 4:11 YHWH accomplished his wrath; he poured out his burning anger.
He kindled a fire in Zion and it devoured her foundations.

Lamed 4:12 The kings of the earth did not believe nor all the inhabitants of the world
That the enemy and the foe came into the gates of Jerusalem.

Mem 4:13 It happened because of[5] the sins of her prophets and the iniquities of her priests
Who poured out in the midst of her the blood of the righteous.

Nun 4:14 Blindly they wandered in the streets, defiled by blood.
No one was able to touch their clothing.

Samek 4:15 "Away, unclean," they called to him, "Away, away, do not touch,
For they depart, indeed, they wander." They said, they shall not dwell among the nations any longer.[6]

Pe 4:16 The face of YHWH scattered them and no longer pays attention to them.
The faces of the priests were not lifted up; the elders were not honored.

God's anger at government and religious leaders is the source of the national catastrophe. YHWH "accomplished his wrath," he completed it, brought it to full intensity, pouring out anger like the fire that destroyed the city to its foundations (4:11). The city's walls, buildings, and temples have been destroyed, but the foundations of the city's social life have crumbled even more thoroughly. In a world where children cannot live, where everyone in the community is afflicted, and where religious leaders' behavior is even worse than the general population, no social life remains. Domestic

---

[5] Following Westermann (1994, 197).

[6] Because this verse is overly long, Hillers (83) and Westermann (1994, 197) believe phrases were added. The verse is difficult, but the sense is clear (Gordis 1974b, 192-193).

and public realms are undermined, and communal foundations are burned away by divine anger.

The narrator imagines kings and inhabitants of the world in astonishment at these things (4:12). The invasion of Jerusalem is unthinkable because it is God's chosen city, specially protected, God's dwelling place, the place of divine rest. The unimaginable has occurred and the world wonders at God's abandonment of the city.

Now the narrator reaches his primary interpretive point (4:13-16)—religious leaders have failed in their responsibilities. Renkema (526) and Westermann (1994, 202-203) insist the leaders' failures are part of the sins of the people, but those are not important to the narrator here. We do not need to harmonize his voice with the book's other poetic voices. In the narrator's accusations against corrupt leaders, he expresses one explanation of the city's fall, but that fall is ultimately multifaceted in its causes.

The prophets sinned and the priests are iniquitous (4:13); more precisely, they poured out "the blood of the righteous" (4:13). This charge, of course, implies murder of the innocent (Renkema 528), but there are metaphoric meanings as well. The "blood of the righteous" may be the city's "life-blood," its economic welfare, torn away by disregard for temple justice (Jer 7:1-8:3). Or, as Provan (117) suggests, the leaders' failure to lead may have encouraged disobedience and blood-spilling by others in the city.

Whatever the priests' offense, the narrator treats blood contamination literally and expounds its consequences in the next few verses (4:14-16). In ancient Israel, defilement by blood made one ritually "unclean," and this contamination by the profane excluded one from worship (Num 19:11-22). To participate in worship, one practiced rites of cleansing, but the narrator does not offer that option. He describes unclean priests and prophets wandering in the streets, as if crazed. Leaders who should see God's ways and God's vision are blind. Priests who are the standard for ritual purity are unclean. No one can touch them, lest they too become unclean, unable to go before God in worship.

Voices call out, "Away, away, do not touch" (4:15). The warning may be shouted by the priests or by the people who send them away in alarm. The guardians of purity have become impure. Like lepers, whose presence was once thought to endanger all, they are about to be expelled from the community and the nations. The failures of prophets and priests contaminate and make profane the entire world.

The narrator ends by returning to his theological interpretation of events (4:11). "The face of YHWH scattered them and no longer pays attention *(nābaṭ)* to them" (4:16a). God's "face" means divine presence, God's being there in person. The phrase calls attention to the deity differently from the name alone—God's very self scattered the priests and prophets and sent them into exile.

And God's very self has stopped paying attention *(nābaṭ)* to them (4:16). Daughter Zion's pleas for God to see and "pay attention" *(nābaṭ,* 1:11c; 2:20a) find a negative echo here, for God no longer notices them and they sink into shame. It is as if the leaders have become invisible and disappeared from God's sight. What remains is only death—the death of children, death from famine, and the death of religious leaders, scattered and hidden from the sight of God. God's anger, burning like fire, is the cause of it all. All has grown dim, dull, exhausted. Survival is bitter—it is better to be dead.

The Community Remembers

As if Zion's people have been standing and listening all along, they now come forward to offer their perspective, or perhaps the narrator speaks in the first-person plural on their behalf (Provan 120). Their speech falls into two parts: Retelling the Invasion (4:17-20) and Future Reversals (4:21-22).

Retelling the Invasion (4:17-20)

'Ayin 4:17 Still our eyes yearned for help in vain.
     We were watching eagerly for a nation that did not save.

Sade 4:18 They hunted our steps so we could not walk in our streets.
     Our end drew near, our days were completed, for our end came.

Qop 4:19 Our pursuers were swifter than the eagles in the heavens.
     They pursued us hotly on the mountains; in the wilderness they lay in wait
     for us.

Res 4:20 Breath of our nostrils,[7] anointed of YHWH, he was taken in their pits,
     Of whom we said, "Under his shadow we will live among the nations."

When abruptly the people begin to speak in these verses, they retell their experience during the invasion. It is the first time that Lamentations speaks of it directly. Until now, speakers have testified about the aftermath of the city's fall and its effects upon them. If they mention the attack at all, it is either a means to convey the survivor's full circumstances or to interpret the assault on the city as a personal action of YHWH (1:10, 21b; 2:16; 3:46).

---

[7] Hillers 77.

By contrast, the community's few words here re-create its collective experience of the invasion itself. Like the narrator, the people speak with economy of emotion. They tell of futile hopes before the attack (4:17), of the enemy's pursuit (4:18-19), and of their loss of hope after the attack (4:20).

Before the invasion their eyes "yearned for help," or perhaps their eyes failed while watching intently for help (4:17). Eyes are prominent in the poem, not weeping eyes of the speakers as in previous chapters (1:2; 2:11, 18; 3:49-51), or eyes of YHWH that will not see (1:9, 11, 20; 2:20; 4:16, but cf. 3:59), but the eyes of a hopeful people, worn out with the strain of looking for help. They watch in vain for "a nation that did not save" (4:17). Whether the search refers to an actual nation such as Egypt, Babylon's only strong opponent, or to another is not clear. But no nation could save them when the attackers are agents of God, though these speakers do not say as much. They simply observe the ineffectiveness of the hoped-for nation.

Unidentified attackers hunt them down (4:18-19). The enemy has invaded their streets, or as the Hebrew suggests, their broad spaces or public squares. The enemy dogged their steps, overtook them, intruded on their public spaces, and hunted them down. The Hebrew repeats "our end" (qiṣṣēnû) near the beginning and at the end of the line (4:18b), as if to emphasize the finality of the city's demise.

"Swifter than eagles" were "our pursuers" (4:19). Like birds of prey, their pursuers fall with incalculable speed and precision upon their quarry. Wherever the people went, to the mountains or the wilderness, the enemy either followed or already lay in wait for them (4:19).

Indication of the nation's end comes in the next verse. The capture of the king, "taken in their pits" (4:20), ends hope and ends the nation. The kings are God's anointed, God's agents upon earth who were to sit upon the throne of Judah forever (2 Sam 7). "Under his shadow we will live among the nations" (4:20), they used to say, but the king's capture ended that hope and the confidence that God would protect them.

The poem closes with a statement of confidence, or perhaps wishful thinking, that the community's suffering will finally abate. Unlike the book's other poems, this one neither speaks to nor petitions God. The absence of petition may express the people's despair and exhaustion, one more example of the dulling and dimming of life among survivors. Or it may seem unnecessary for the speakers to appeal to God, since they express confidence that Zion's punishment has ended (4:22). But the presence of chapter 5 adds another possibility. The people continue to speak in the book's final poem and address God alone with a petition that may complete the complaint begun in chapter 4. Chapter 4 does not petition God because chapter 5 does. Because all the poems lack stage directions and linking devices, this view is no more than an interpretive hunch. What is certain is that chapter 4 stands alone as the acrostic shortens, grows thematically thinner, emotionally less intense, and, by itself, ignores God.

Future Reversals (4:21-22)

Sin 4:21   Rejoice and be glad, Daughter Edom, you who live in the land of Uz,
       But to you will pass the cup. You will become drunk and strip yourself naked.

Taw 4:22   Your punishment[8] is accomplished, Daughter Zion; he will not continue to exile you.
       Your iniquity, Daughter Edom, he will observe with care; he will uncover your sins.

The survivors now turn to the Daughter of Edom, as if the capital city of the neighboring nation were standing at the gate waiting for conversation. In these verses Edom's fate encircles and frames the fate of Zion as they exchange places in the poetry if not yet in the world's political realities. Mockingly, the speakers command their neighbors to rejoice and celebrate. The prophet Obadiah, whose entire book is an accusation against Edom, charges that nation with treachery against Judah when it was under attack (Raabe 207-243). Like Zion, the poetry personifies Edom as a "daughter" who is soon to disgrace herself by stripping herself naked. Though she may rejoice now, "the cup" of wrath will pass to her, and she will suffer as Zion has suffered. Once again the shaming of the female body symbolizes the dissolution of public honor.

The cup from which Daughter Edom will drink is no ordinary cup—it is the cup of wrath that Jeremiah passes among the nations to symbolize their collapse (Jer 25:15-29). Judah and Jerusalem will drink of it first, and then all the enemy nations will drink in turn. They will each become drunk, vomit, stagger, go out of their minds, and fall to rise no more (Jer 25:16, 27). The cup of wrath is a metaphor that presents the rise and fall of nations as divinely directed and shameful punishment for sin. Wine, judged to be a boon to humanity in other texts, is here a poison.

But Daughter Zion will be restored as Edom falls. Verb forms show the interconnected fates of the two nations. God will not continue to exile *(gālah)* Zion; God will uncover *(gālah)* Edom's sins (4:22). Hillers (91) finds these verses to be the most hopeful in the book because they point to an end of

---

[8] *'Awônēk* is used in both lines of the verse and can mean "punishment" and "iniquity" (see 4:6).

Zion's suffering, or at least imply that the invasion was the climax of divine wrath. Amelioration of pain must surely follow. Yet the whole section appears to be spoken in the style of curses and blessings that have a tenuous quality about them. In the future, things will get better (Provan 123), but that future may be distant indeed.

The community gloats over the future pain of its enemies. Strangely, the enemies under the promises of vengeance are not the Babylonians. Although the Edomite reference is not easily explained, the bitter desire for vengeance is understandable. To suggest that the people have learned little from their experience of invasion and occupation because they hope for vengeance is to misunderstand the nature of laments and to deny normal response to trauma, catastrophe, and subjection. Hatred and wishes for vengeance against cruel and oppressive enemies are typical and normal human responses to trauma. The ethical dilemma appears when people begin to act upon those desires. This poem brings the community's response into the open, creating psychic and spiritual space to begin imagining another reality, a different future.

6

Plea from an Occupied Land

Lamentations 5

By the time we reach the final poem, we are ready for respite, for hope, for some indication that new life is over the horizon, waiting in this chapter. But in this "house for sorrow" no happy ending awaits the occupants. Grief and anger, doubt and despair have taken up residence and will not be evicted. No premature solutions intrude upon the pain that many would like to ban from life, from consciousness, from prayer. In this final poem, God does not speak, the people do not acquire hope, and comfort eludes them. The book tells truth about profound suffering by its realistic literary shape that refuses to place hope at the end (Brunet 83).

The whole of chapter 5 is a petition spoken in the first-person voice of the people. The petition demands God's attention (5:1; 5:19-22) and encloses a complaint (5:2-18), telling God what to pay attention to—the wretchedness of life in the occupied land. Like so much of the book, the people's prayer is bleak, bitter, and hopeless (5:2-18), and it ends haltingly with an ambiguous plea for God to act (5:19-22).

A Shorter, Less Structured Poem

Chapter 5 contains the book's shortest poem and the only one that is not an acrostic. It is, however, alphabetic because it contains twenty-two verses, the same number of verses as letters in the Hebrew alphabet. The shortening of the poem, the absence of the acrostic, and the ambiguity of the final verses raise interpretive questions. Why does the book's final poem become even shorter than chapter 4 and then abandon the acrostic altogether? And why does the book end on such a sour, despairing note? To answer these questions in the past, interpreters speculated that each poem existed independently before being complied into a loose anthology with little arrangement or coherence. But with several contemporary interpreters (Dobbs-Alsopp, Renkema, Linafelt 2001, Provan, and Joyce 1999), I assume Lamentations to be a carefully crafted work of art and that the variations in form and length express meanings.

Lanahan thinks the absence of the acrostic form in chapter 5 indicates a divine shrinking from punishment that is a certainty extending from A to Z in the previous acrostics. But the tragedy or "punishment" has already occurred from the book's first chapter. Lamentation's relinquishment of the acrostic in chapter 5, instead, signifies an abandonment of efforts to contain suffering within a recognizable alphabetic order. Even as the alphabetic length of the poem links it to the book's earlier acrostic poems, its divergence from them may also imply accelerating hopelessness in accord with the poem's increasingly hopeless contents.

The poems lines are short and lack the *qinah* meter. Verses punch at us with quick force, partly because they contain more precise parallelism than the earlier poems, wherein the verse's second part closely echoes the first. All these poetic devices of shortened forms suggest the depletion of hope and energy, as if the community has no feeling left, only enough life for understated description and for a last stab at winning God's attention.

The desolation previous poems sought to contain by poetic structures breaks loose here. Chapter 5 recounts atrocities of life in the occupied land. Everything that constitutes common life has come undone. Physical necessities, personal safety, honor, and human dignity—all have buckled and collapsed along with the city's buildings and walls. And the community's relationship with God seems irreparably damaged.

The final poem forms part of an overall structure that echoes with exquisite honesty the flowing and ebbing of energy among survivors. Lamentations' first three chapters are of equal length, although the third heightens the acrostic and brings the poetry to a climax of anger, grief, and hope. Chapter 4 blunts this climax. Its voices are more distant and its forms abbreviated compared to the earlier poems. Chapter 5 becomes even shorter and less structured still. Its diminished length and abandonment of the acrostic imply a numbing, recurring despair among survivors and leave the book without closure. But that refusal of resolution enables the book in its turbulence, conflict, and confusion to portray pain without compromise.

Pain without Compromise

Together the poems enact various responses to the tragedy. The poems' many voices, acrostic and alphabetic structures, hybrid genres, and uneven

lengths echo tensions, conflicts, and fractured meanings common in literature of survival (Linafelt 2000). They set clashing viewpoints next to each
other. They move through a range of emotions and theological positions
and simply leave them. The book's poems are like a tightly wound electrical
wire that frays into short threads at the end, no longer able to contain its
burden as its outside casing falls away.

The final poem divides into two sections: What God Should See (5:1-18)
and What God Should Do (5:19-22).

What God Should See (5:1-18)

5:1   Remember, YHWH, what has happened to us; pay attention and see our
        shame.

5:2   Our inheritance is turned over to strangers, our houses to foreigners.

5:3   Orphans we have become, without fathers; our mothers have become like
        widows.

5:4   We must pay for the water we drink; the wood we get must be bought at a
        price.[1]

5:5   We are pursued up to our neck; we are weary and receive no rest.[2]

5:6   We have given a hand to Egypt and Assyria to get enough bread.

5:7   Our ancestors sinned and are no more; we bear their guilt.

5:8   Servants rule over us; no one tears us from their hands.

5:9   We get our bread at danger of our lives because of the sword in the wilder-
        ness.

5:10   Our skin is like a scorched pot from the fever heat of famine.

5:11   Women in Zion are raped, virgins in the cities of Judah.

5:12   Princes are hung by their hands; faces of the elders are not honored.

---

[1] See Provan (126) and see the *New Jerusalem Bible* translation.
[2] The text is corrupt and often emended to read: "With a yoke upon our neck
we are hard driven" (NRSV). See Provan's (126-127) detailed discussion.

5:13   Young men bear the burden of the grinding mill; boys stagger under loads of wood.

5:14   Elders have departed from the gate, young men from their music.

5:15   Our hearts have ceased from joy; our dancing has been overturned by mourning.

5:16   The crown has fallen from our heads; woe to us for we have sinned.

5:17   Because of this our hearts grew faint; because of these things our eyes have grown dark.

5:18   Upon Mount Zion lies desolation; jackals prowl upon it.[3]

The communal voice urges, insists, and demands. Three imperative verbs dominate the opening line, stating plainly what the speakers want from YHWH. They want God to "remember" *(zākar),* to "pay attention" *(nābaṭ),* and to "see" *(rā'āh).* The request for God to remember, new in this book, involves more than intellectual recall of past events. The community pleads with God to "remember what has happened" (5:1) to bring its tragedy completely and experientially to mind. It calls God to bring their suffering alive and to reenter it in the present. Whether the people want God to remember the past invasion and city's collapse or their current, desperate existence is not clear; for them it is imperative that God bring their suffering into consciousness. But rather than remembering, God has forgotten their "shame" (5:1). The people know they are out of God's sight and God's mind.

This poem emerges from a past that dominates the present, but it does not refer to it. Rather it attends narrowly to the overwhelming violence and desolation of ordinary life in the present. The people struggle mightily to survive, and it is this that God must see. Like previous speakers, they hope that God's seeing might provoke action on their behalf. But because God does not see, God compounds their pain. Cast off and disregarded, they have become invisible and utterly insignificant to God.

The speakers want God to see a devastated world (5:2-18). In a flat intoning of their reality, they describe the destruction of their living space (5:2-5), and interrupt the catalogue of terrors only briefly to blame their

---

[3] With Provan (132) and Hiller (96), I understand verse 18 as a summary of the complaint rather than a causative statement (Renkema 620; Westermann 1994, 209-210).

ancestors for their suffering (5:7). Then they return to the material conditions of quotidian life in the destroyed city (5:8-18). There is no talk here of the city's past glories or of its once exalted circumstances; their vision has shrunk to the immediate bodily needs of food and safety.

With vivid snapshots of occupation, the poetry depicts life at its most devastated. Every realm of the people's space is invaded and intruded upon, and the difficulties of survival dominate their speech. Their first complaint summarizes their situation: "Our inheritance is turned over to strangers, our houses to foreigners" (5:2). Their "inheritance" is the land God gave them, now controlled by strangers and foreigners; they have no safe place in it. Homeless in their own land and deprived of room for living, their bodily survival is in doubt. Emotional and spiritual needs hardly matter in this struggle for life.

Not only is their physical space occupied by others, their family life no longer exists. They have "become orphans" because there are no fathers (5:3). Mothers have "become like widows" (5:3); like the city woman herself (1:1b), they are husbandless, childless, and futureless. Foreign invaders and occupiers of the land crowd out families of protection, care, and nurturing, and endanger orphans and widows they created in the first place.

Necessities that sustain daily life are nearly beyond reach. People must pay for water and wood, without which they cannot cook or keep warm (5:4). They live under continual threat; "we are pursued up to our neck" (5:5). This verse is difficult in Hebrew and may indicate that the survivors must do forced labor (5:13). Many commentators emend verse 5 to read, "With a yoke upon our necks we are hard driven." A yoke is a traditional image of slavery, and in conditions of foreign occupation, economic enslavement is likely, but the Hebrew does not say that without alteration.

What is clear is that the people live under far-reaching and unrelenting threat. They are "up to their necks" and cannot find safety or rest. Facing constant menace, their bodies and spirits are worn down by weariness, and life has thinned and shriveled to the level of subsistence. These speakers might agree with the narrator's words in the previous chapter: "Better off those pierced by the sword than those pierced by hunger" (4:9). Better to be dead than to waste away slowly, they might think despairingly.

The dehumanization of the people is under way. To survive, they have sold their souls. To obtain bread, they have come to the aid of Egypt and Assyria, literally "given a hand to" those nations (5:6). They have exchanged loyalty for food. Egypt and Assyria are former invaders of Israel, and to be in alliance with them meant to promise allegiance to their gods. Because the speakers are in no position to aid or make alliances with other nations, Egypt and Assyria probably symbolize the current invaders to whom the speakers have sold their souls in order to eat and survive (Provan 128). Alternatively, the verse may refer to sins of the ancestors mentioned but unspecified in the next verse who did make alliances with Egypt and Assyria (Hillers 104; Renkema 602). Whether the reference to the nations is symbolic or historic, the people understand relationship with them as a sell-out for food. They are profoundly disquieted by what they must do to live.

"Our ancestors sinned and are no more; we bear their guilt" (5:7). Since the community is one living entity, the sins of the previous generations bleed over into the present world (5:6). Whatever those sins might be, they threaten the present generation. Yet the speakers may be distancing themselves from parental guilt by claiming that the ancestors' failures, not theirs, set the nation on its course to the catastrophe. But this poem does not linger over the question of the guilt, though it will return to it later (5:16). Instead, they tell of the effects of occupation upon communal life.

Peril All Around

Degradation and terror surround members of the community in the next verses (5:8-14). The spare, short lines convey a sense of the huge effort and caution needed for survival as they search for food, safety, and warmth in the face of constant attacks. Servants replace royal descendants of the house of David as rulers of the nation. "Servants rule over us; no one tears us from their hands" (5:8). Not only is their own king, symbol of the nation and head of their government, no longer on the throne, but servants rule them. Servants are generally not educated or prepared for governance; in the eyes of the speakers, right relationships have been inverted in the society. Hillers (105) thinks that the servants are Babylonian officials (cf. 2 Kings 25:24), perhaps especially lowly and brutal ones, or the new rulers may be former servants in Jerusalem now collaborating with the enemy. Incompetence, insult, and brutality may all be at issue here, particularly since no one "tears" the people from this rule.

Struggles for survival occur at the most fundamental level. Even obtaining food and bread is life threatening. Procuring basic needs of daily living imperils human life because of the "sword in the wilderness" (5:9), perhaps referring to the occupying military force or the ravages of drought and famine. Historical conditions are uncertain, but the poem does not seek to present history. It conveys by symbol, suggestion, and connotation the survivors' predicament; current conditions fiercely endanger life. The very act of acquiring food to nourish life itself threatens to destroy life.

Struggles for food are only the beginning. The speakers complain that their skin looks like a burnt cooking pot from the fevers among them (5:10).

Then, using third-person speech, they turn to the fates of various groups within the community (5:11-14). Women are raped in the city, as are virgins in other towns of Judah. As happens in all wars, women are the spoils, and their violation is a weapon of insult and destruction against the entire people. In the ancient world, the rape of women had little importance as an offense against women themselves. Instead, it was a tactic of humiliation and subjugation of the men who should protect them. It attacked the nation's "purity" in the mixing of peoples, and it attempted to eradicate the bloodlines of the people. The particular pain of women finds no expression in this verse.

Dehumanizing of the community continues. The occupiers torture and hang princes and dishonor and shame elders (5:12-13). As members of the royal family, the princes represent the entire people; elders are the bedrock of the community who act as conduits of tradition and judges in legal matters. The invaders force young men to labor at the grinding mill, supposedly the work of slave women (Renkema 612). Boys stagger under loads of wood too burdensome for their weakened bodies. The assaults on the people are physical, but the occupier simultaneously attacks their humanity, their forms of governance, and their communal arrangements. There is nothing left to them but an instinctive drive to live.

Precise conditions, consequences, and meanings of each verse are left ambiguous and suggestive rather than detailed. The poetry does not explain matters, but in a rhetoric of expanding fear, shows snippets of life that convey the extent and totality of destruction. Legal and social interchange has ended—the elders no longer sit in the gates. Young men no longer play their music, for worship and youthful joy have ended (5:14). There is no safety, no place left for communal or domestic life, and no room for normal roles and behavior.

The people report the impact of the tragedy on their spirits (5:15-18): "Our hearts have ceased from joy" and "our dancing has been overturned by mourning" (5:15). As Jeremiah prophesied, joy and dancing have disappeared from the land (Jer 7:34; 16:9). Sorrow prevails for "the crown has fallen from our heads" (5:16). Once a proud nation, they now have neither monarchy nor independence. They no longer live in dignity and comfort like royalty but have become like slaves and servants. Because the crown has fallen, because they have sinned, their "hearts grew faint." Limp with mourning, their "eyes have grown dark" (5:17); they have lost hope and courage; they have no future to imagine and no food to eat. God's eyes do not see them, so they, in turn, cannot see either political or domestic space for survival.

The final line of their complaint summarizes their conditions. "Upon Mount Zion lies desolation; jackals prowl upon it" (5:18). In every facet of

its being, their city and the abundant life it once contained lie abandoned
and destroyed. Like an empty and decaying house, the city is fit only for
prowling beasts. Though people may still live there, their existence is precarious, and the occupiers continuously assault their very humanity. Social
and cultural life no longer exist, their physical beings are attacked, and the
crown has fallen. Once full of people, Zion has become like a widow (1:1).
Jackals prowl through the city. One hope remains for this community, and
that hope is exceedingly thin.

What God Should Do (5:19-22)

5:19   You,[4] YHWH, sit upon your throne forever, from generation to genera-
        tion.[5]

5:20   Why have you forgotten us forever? Why have you abandoned us these
        many days?

5:21   Return us to yourself, YHWH, and we will return; renew our days as of
        old,

5:22   Unless[6] you have utterly rejected us and you are angry with us forever.

We might entitle the people's final prayer, "What God Should Do But
Probably Will Not." Their address to God is startling, in part because they
use the independent personal pronoun you *('atāh)* even though they could
express direct address without it. The pronoun is an attention-getting device, an emphatic appeal to awaken God's notice and to make a personal
connection with God, as if to say, "You, YHWH, no one else, only you, the
one who rules from generation to generation" (5:19).

Mention of divine rule is a form or praise, a public recognition of honor
due to the deity. But it is also a form of beseeching by praise, a manipula-
tion, a flattery, as if to get on God's good side, so perhaps God might listen.
It is God's rule that has put them in this desolate world where jackals prowl.
The people's double-edged praise slides over immediately into challenge. "Why
have you forgotten us forever? Why have you abandoned us these many days?"
(5:20). They move from blaming themselves and their ancestors (15:7, 16b)

---

    [4] Hillers (100) says "but or yet" is suggested by the personal pronoun and its
prominent position.
    [5] So also Renkema.
    [6] For discussion of the possibilities of translation, see Gordis (1974a); but Provan
(133-134) and Linafelt (2001b) have the best conclusion.

to blaming God in these final verses. God failed them, forgot them, and abandoned them, and they demand to know why. They want a broad view of their predicament, a way to cope with it, understand it and move beyond it.

The people ask for double-edged movement in their relationship, that God return *(šûb)* to them and they return *(šûb)* to God (5:21). With the verb of turning, the speakers demand restoration of covenant relationship and renewal of life. Like Daughter Zion, they omit requests for the return of past glories and the good old days. They want something far deeper, something primal. They ask for a turning around of God, for a conversion of God's heart back to them. They want God to turn from abandoning and rejecting them.

And they themselves want to return to God. They want their relationship restored, as if they and God had walked away from each other and can now turn back and begin anew. But God's turning is what matters, for they have been turning to God throughout the book. God holds the power in this relationship, and God must take the initiative now. They have shown God the pall of death over their lives, how pitiful are the conditions of their children, elders, princes, and young women, and the jackals roaming through their city and across their spirits. They ask for a future, a new life, and restored relations with God, relations that have been so disrupted that they cannot even get God to look toward them. They ask for more than bodily survival; they want to live, flourish, and be made new.

It would be good if the book ended here, if it closed on the request typical of many laments—positive, hopeful, and edging toward confidence that they and God might begin again. Instead, the people close their prayer with a dispirited modification of their request: "Return us to yourself . . . unless you have utterly rejected us and are angry with us forever" (5:21-22). This verse has driven translators to their lexicons, concordances, and other ancient versions in search of a more positive translation. Hillers (100-101) and Linafelt (2001b) delineate numerous possible translations, ranging from turning the line into a question, "Or have you utterly rejected us?" (Westermann 1994, 210), to making God's rejection a past event over and done with, "Even though you greatly despised us and had been angry with us!" (Gordis 1974b, 151).

But the book's final verse yields a happy ending only by distorting the Hebrew text (Linafelt 2001; Provan 133-134; Hillers 100-101). The crux of the translation problem is the introductory phrase "*kî 'im*." The phrase means literally "for if," "unless," "except"; that is, the phrase introduces conditions. If we read it that way the poem will not allow us to force a settled ending on it, or what Gordis calls "a vigorous, clear, and appropriate conclusion to the penitential prayer" (1974b, 198). But chapter 5 is not a penitential prayer—it is a demand that God see the people's pain and the conclusion is most appropriate.

The text expresses the community's doubt about God's care and about God's character. It utters the unthinkable—that God has utterly and permanently rejected them, cast them off in unrelenting anger. The verse is fearsome, a nightmare of abandonment, like a child's terror that the only ones who can protect her and give her a home have rejected her forever. Such is the ending of this book, and I think it is wonderful.

It is wonderful because it is truthful, because it does not force hope prematurely, because it expresses what many in worlds of trauma and destruction know to be true. Its very unsettledness enables the book to be a house for sorrow, neither denied nor overcome with sentimental wishes, theological escapism, or premature closure. Although Lamentations does not tell the whole story and does not contain all there is to say about God's relationship to the world, it does tell truth about the human experience of suffering.

Unsettled Longing

The poetic voices of the book of Lamentations work upon the reader. Characters, suggested more than portrayed, move back and forth over the same psychic, physical, and spiritual grounds. They illustrate different features of the landscape of hunger, torture, shame, and abandonment. They agree that God must look, see, pay attention, and remember them. They never receive a reply. The poem in the book's center arrives at hope haltingly, with a tentativeness that makes it precarious and fragile. Hope is one voice among several, one moment of survival, one glimpse beyond torment, captivity, and desolation. The book does not sustain that hope—it cannot. To do so would be to lie, to cover over, to deny the reality of the survivor's longing for God's missing voice. With thinning hope and flagging energy, the voices drift away.

PART II

Reflections

A Theology of Witness

7

The Power of the Missing Voice

Lamentations is a book of shifting voices. Nancy Lee calls it a "performance," a dramatization of speakers who bear witness in the style of folkloric writing. We can imagine the speakers gathered in a public place; they stand up, each in turn, to tell of their particular pain and demand God's attention. Each voice embodies some aspect of the suffering that belongs to the whole community. In this chapter I discuss the reverence the book accords to voices of the afflicted, the necessity of honoring voices of pain for human flourishing, and the power of God's missing voice.

Voices refer to the literary device of speaking personae in Lamentations, but they are also a metaphor. They signify the emergence of human capacity to act in the world by bringing pain to speech (Scarry 33). To gain a voice means to come into the truth of one's history corporately and individually, to recover one's life, to acquire moral agency by naming one's world. The voice brings from the depths of silence the creative power, energy, and wholeness of a person or a people in the midst of its world. Central to feminist and liberationist thought, the metaphor of the voice evokes aspirations of many in the neo-colonial world of global capitalism. Rather than be spoken for, peoples seek to assert their voices to "represent themselves rather than being represented, or, in the worst cases, rather than being effaced" (Frank 13).

Many Views of Tragedy

Speakers in Lamentations express a plurality of theologies and interpretations that yields no single understanding of their common tragedy. They are not debating or trying to refute each other; rather, their testimonies nudge up against each other in disquieting tension and conflict. They bring the "unspeakable" to expression in incomplete ways, and they seek and speak about God in a similar limited fashion. Each testimony is narrow and occluded, yet compelling. No voice wins out, unifies, or dominates the claims of other voices. The strongman's hopeful voice does not silence other voices, but neither do the others overpower his hope. All perspectives remain together in churning, unsettled interaction.

In its turmoil, Lamentations embodies postmodern understandings of truth. The term *postmodern* is slippery, allowing many interpretations. At the least, it reflects a loss of confidence in theories, theologies, and viewpoints that claim to speak for everyone and seek to compel agreement from everyone, no matter his or her circumstances in the world (McKnight 27-65; Brueggemann 1993, 1-25). Postmodernism asserts that no single voice, theory, or theology is able to encompass the multiplicity of human experience. Our grasp on truth is partial, limited, and conditioned by our concrete lives. The voices of Lamentations speak from particular and limited perspectives. The book honors each by not resolving them into a unified vision, and it treats these multiple voices of pain as hallowed ground.

One voice is conspicuously absent from Lamentations. The most authoritative of biblical figures, the only speaker who could proclaim light, hope, and a future in these circumstances, is missing. God does not speak, does not respond, does not heal, does not "see." The book's deepest yearning is for the missing voice, the Absent One, the God who hides behind clouds (3:43).

Across the poems, speakers direct our eyes and our hope toward the deity; they long for God sorrowfully, angrily, and despairingly. They play upon readers' own longings for comfort, for explanation, for even the slightest response. Their pleas open a space for divine response, but God never comes into the emptiness. Instead, the space remains vacant and opaque, leaving a well of unrealized longing.

For survivors of Jerusalem's fall, God's silence signifies what Arthur Frank would call "narrative wreckage" (Frank 54). The story of their relationship with God was wrecked the way news of cancer suddenly interrupts and destroys the story of a life. The God who rescued them from slavery, who brought them to the promised land, who chose to dwell with them on Mount Zion, and who gave David and his descendants the throne forever (2 Sam 7) has abandoned them. Now nothing remains of their mutual story but a ruined city through which the jackals prowl (5:18).

When a people's symbolic narrative collapses, they "cannot move toward the future" (Schreiter 31; Joyce 1993, 310). They have neither plan nor rudder with which to guide their steps, claim their identity, and provide safety. God's silence in Lamentations greatly exacerbates their suffering because it signifies the end of life as they have known it. Without God, without their story, they have no future. After worlds collapse, survivors need a new story or what Reynolds Price calls in the title of his book "a whole new life." After a devastating struggle with spinal cancer, Price realized his former narrative—a story of bodily health, mobility, and sense of himself as a vigorous person—was irretrievably gone. In its place he needed a new way of imagining life, a new story that could guide him within the bounds of his physical constraints.

Lamentations marks out the place of ruptured life, when the old story fails and a new one has yet to appear, as well it might (Frank 169-185). Only because God's voice is missing can the book symbolize this vacuum of meaning, this liminal world of impasse, this time when the old life has ended and no new imaginings are yet possible.

Inspired Restraint

The silence of God in Lamentations is inspired. By this I mean it shows a brilliant restraint that breathes power into the book. If God were to speak, what could God say? If you were charged to write God's speech for the book, a luminous chapter 6, what would you write? How would you write it? What form would you give it? Would you resume the acrostic? Would your voice of God explain and apologize, chide and accuse, or comfort and heal? Literary and theological difficulties abound, but for skilled and gifted poets of the spirit, they are not insurmountable.

Israel's writers had resources to help them bring God to speech if they wanted to do so. In Mesopotamian laments over the fallen cities, the gods speak and sometimes return and restore the city (Dobbs-Allsopp 1993, 92-94). In a few biblical laments, God speaks (Pss 60:7-8; 108:7-8); God replies directly in two laments of Jeremiah (Jer 11:18-12:6; 15:10-21) and after Job's long, bitter laments (Job 38:1-41:34).

God's speechlessness in Lamentations must be a calculated choice, a conscious theological decision, an inspired control by the book's composers, for how could a response from the deity do anything but ruin the book? The strongman's hope (chap. 3) shows what happens to sorrow, doubt, and anger when even tentative and faltering hope appears. Readers and interpreters, Jewish and Christian alike, cling to his words, as if these few hopeful passages were the only words in the book (Linafelt 2000). Anger and grief, absence and doubt slide into the interpretive margins, smothered and silenced by hope.

No matter what God said, Lamentations would come to premature resolution, and the book's capacity to house sorrow would dissipate. Any words from God would endanger human voices. They would undercut anger and despair, foreshorten protest, and give the audience only a passing glimpse of the real terror of their condition. Divine speaking would trump all speech.

The missing voice of God leaves suffering exposed. In the language of poet Nelly Sachs, it creates an opening between "the rocks of yesterday and tomorrow, held apart like the rims of a wound" (Sachs 220-221). God's silence in Lamentations leaves wounds festering, open to the air and possibly to healing. The benefit of exposed wounds is that they become visible and unavoidable. Left exposed, they require us to see, acknowledge, and attend to them, and then perhaps there can be energy to attend to the wounds of the world.

Lamentations' haunting power lies in its brutal honesty about the Missing Voice; its brilliance is that it does not speak for God. God's frightening silence is resonant with interpretive possibility. It makes of the poetry a haven for voices of pain. It prevents us from sliding prematurely over suffering toward happy endings. It gives the book daring power because it honors human speech. God's absence forces us to attend to voices of grief and despair, and it can reflect, vividly or remotely, our own experiences of a silent God. Surprisingly, the book does express hope, but only in the unsteady, halting, and tenuous way known to survivors of cataclysm, trauma, depression, or loss. Hope appears and disappears, elusive as the future itself. If God spoke, God's words would diminish the voices of pain, wash over them, and crowd them out. Even one word from God would take up too much space in the book.

By leaving conflicting voices in unresolved tension, staying stubbornly in the space of pain, suffering, and collapse, Lamentations offers a way to articulate suffering and insists on the need to do so. Only the silence of God enables the book to "face squarely the matters of suffering and death" (Linafelt 2000, 26) and to insist on the sheer fact of pain. Because God does not speak, the book focuses relentlessly on the wreckage that occurred in Zion.

Because God's voice is missing, Lamentations honors truth-telling and denies "denial." Human speech about suffering matters so much that Lamentations presents it in all its rawness. It lingers over pain and gives words to mute suffering. A house for sorrow and a school for compassion, it teaches resistance, liberates passions, and gives us prayers for the world's tears. These may be enormous claims for so small a book. Yet by honoring the voices of suffering, the book undermines familial and cultural systems that deny it.

Denying Pain

Fear of truth motivates its denial. Denial refers to the refusal, perhaps even the psychic and spiritual inability, to see the horrible, to name it, to allow it space in the world. Denial means to live knowingly or unknowingly with lies. In both psychological and political terms, denial can be a survival tactic, a banishing of events too shattering to face. It can be a way to stay alive and to continue to function in the face of horrible events. Judith Lewis Herman writes: "The typical response to atrocity and trauma is to banish them from consciousness. Certain violations of the social contract are too terrible to allow them to come to consciousness or to be uttered aloud" (Herman 7). This, she says, is "the meaning of the word *unspeakable.*" As a response to an immediate crisis, denial—or put another way, selective amnesia—can be a healthy response to radical suffering.

But when denial becomes a hardened way of life, it inhibits human flourishing, cuts off the spirit at its roots, silences voices, and blocks passion for justice. Whether practiced by societies or individuals, denial constricts hope, depletes life, and aborts praise. Crushed spirits cannot worship unless that worship speaks from the pain.

With theological abandon, I have come to think of denial as original sin, a primal human rejection of the truth.

> [God] said, "Who told you that you were naked? Have you eaten from the tree of which I commanded you not to eat?" The man said, "The woman whom you gave to be with me, she gave me fruit from the tree, and I ate." Then the LORD God said to the woman, "What is this you have done?" The woman said, "The serpent tricked me, and I ate." (Gen 3:11-13, NRSV)

To God's accusing questions, neither man nor woman answers with truth. Hiding in the garden of paradise, both lack the courage to see or admit the hiding of their spirits. They fear the truth, so they deny, lie, and accuse, and the result is the fracturing of all relationships in paradise. Humans are cut off from their own bodies, from each other, from the animals, from God, and from the earth itself.

Could the story in the garden end differently, if the woman and the man answered honestly? I imagine each looking God in the eye and saying, "I ate from the forbidden tree," and God saying, "I told you not to, but I see you have grown up. I see you take responsibility for your lives, so I leave you in charge of the garden. Work it out together." Would cosmic harmony replace the couple's alienation from everything and everyone? Would God have extended a different future to the mythic couple and the world if they had courageously named what they denied? Or is the illusion of paradise too lovely to risk by speaking truth?

Just as denial in the garden pollutes relationships with self, others, the earth, and God, so denial in personal life directly affects social and political life. Despite the sharp dualism that separates personal and social life in Western cultures, boundaries between the two realms are porous. Carolyn Forché is adamant that false distinctions between the personal and the social constrict life in both realms.

> The distinction between the personal and the political gives the political realm too much and too little scope; at the same time, it renders the personal too important and not important enough. If we give up the dimension of the personal, we risk relinquishing one of the most powerful sites of resistance. The celebration of the personal, however, can indicate a myopia, an inability to see how larger structures of the economy and the state circumscribe, if not determine, the fragile realm of individuality. (Forché 31)

Forché's analysis aptly names the cost of maintaining the vast chasm between the individual and the society. Yet this distinction, so deeply entrenched in the culture, pervades some churches, missionary and spirituality movements, and groups working for justice. The "celebration of the personal" in its extremes of selfishness and myopia contributes to the "covert despair of the affluent" (Hall) because it cuts us off from others. But equally harmful are countering efforts that focus solely on social, political, and economic conditions. Too often efforts that diminish or deny the personal in favor of social engagements squander personal energies for the works of justice and reconciliation, shut down sources of resistance, and risk distortions of vision.

Instead of dividing the personal and political, the individual and communal, we need theological and spiritual ways of being in the world that recognize the porous nature of boundaries between the individual and society. Lamentations can be a resource in this work because it invites personal and social truth-telling that can release passions and encourage moral agency. It teaches compassion. Until those of us who care for the well-being of the earth and its peoples come to terms with our own pain, we are unlikely to be able to receive the suffering of others on their terms. Until we, the people of the only remaining superpower, recognize our own hidden despair, we will not be able to receive the tears of the world and to see our complicity in them.

When more than 80 percent of the world's population suffer immensely arduous lives and eke out only a tenuous subsistence, while we reside in excess—sometimes obscene excess—then illness and inhumanity swallow us all. I am not so naive as to think that overcoming collective denial of our true condition will alter these profound inequities, but I am certain that there is no way forward until we see them.

The Family as School of Denial

Just as the family is the first school of injustice (Young; hooks 2000, 20), it is also the first school of denial; it was for me. Despite living in a laughing, loving family, I have long carried within me an emotional and spiritual world that resonated with Lamentations' radical suffering. As culture critic bell hooks insists about herself, my own academic work has been "a psychoanalytic project" (hooks 1994, 209), and Lamentations has been one of my companions through a long process of self-reclamation.

My expressive, loving family practiced denial. It forbade anger, ignored sorrow, and created a culture of silence about hard things. From generation to generation, we practiced denial: we looked on the bright side, walked on the sunny side, and remembered that tomorrow is a new day. Like many assimilating immigrant groups, deaths went ungrieved, anger lurked but could not speak, and broken dreams were barely noticed. Some of us lost great chunks of ourselves in the process.

Alice Miller describes how denial originates even in "the good home." She writes about traditional child-rearing practices in Europe and the United States, and speaks not only of damage to children from physical abuse, but also of the soul-crushing effects of emotional abuse and neglect. Often loving parents violate the child's well-being with well-intentioned disciplinary practices. Miller tells of her own domination by a mother who would praise her academic achievements but "ignore her for days on end to reduce her to subservience" and "teach her a lesson" (Miller 1991, 19) for her own good.

Such treatment causes children to fixate on achievements in order to keep the parent's love. Typically, the children blame themselves for this cruelty— "I am not good enough," "I deserved it," "I'll try harder"—because blaming the parents upon whom their welfare depends is unthinkable. Thus begin cycles of guilt and shame. Miller calls such battering of children a form of "psychic murder" (1991, 83). To cope with parental ignorance and abuse, children often build protective emotional walls that seal off their pain even from themselves. They may be completely unaware of the dynamic, but in adulthood they often experience anguish that seems without cause; the emotions survive though the memories are lost.

When they seek to understand their reality, friends and family may urge them to leave the past in the past—"What's done is done" or "Why bring that up again?" But when denial's protective walls seal away the past, the neglected child still lives, abandoned and betrayed. The 1999 film "Magnolia" makes this point with vignettes of several broken lives loosely joined by the repeated refrain, "You may be finished with the past, but the past is not finished with you."

As adults, such children need the hidden truth of the past. They need to bring their suffering to light to regain selves, to take possession of their own voices, to become true moral agents. In Miller's view, society needs this as well, because the destructive behavior of criminals and tyrants emerges in part from repression of the pain of childhood abuse. Because Lamentations articulates and honors pain, it can be a companion for people living in enforced silence.

Global Society and Hopelessness

A group of international theologians called the Campbell Scholars gathered at Columbia Theological Seminary to discuss the theme of hope. They discern in the present global society "a pervasive loss, diminution, or distortion of hope," but in North American culture they find that despair is insidiously "covert." A sense of futility and hopelessness "masquerades under a guise of well-being so persuasive as to deceive the wearers of the mask themselves." This hidden despair rises up when a system of meaning disintegrates, and it expresses itself in violence against the other and the world, a violence necessary to maintain the denial. Only a new sense of meaning can replace false hopes and artificial meanings that keep the lid on the despair itself. The despair of the affluent differs from that of the dispossessed because the latter do not have the luxury of denial; their concrete conditions make denial impossible.

> To be poor, hungry, ill-clad, inadequately sheltered or in other ways physically deprived; to be at the mercy of gross economic injustice, ethnic violence, and political chaos; to be rejected or marginalized on account of race, gender, class, ethnicity, sexual orientation, etc.: such conditions not only leave little space for the luxury of repression, they represent an actualization here and now of the "shock" that possessing peoples are able to relegate to an indefinite future. (Hall)

Anyone who has lived or worked among the afflicted and their advocates knows that remarkable hope is often found among them, precisely because they cannot avoid facing the depth of their predicament. Like the hope of the strongman in chapter 3 of Lamentations, this dynamic is biblical. Hope, "when it is authentic, arises out of the crucible of hopelessness—that is, is always in some sense hope against hope" (Rom 4:18; Hall).

Life in the United States contains many blessings of peace, prosperity, and freedom and seems to be a place where Lamentations need not detain us. But for many, enormous wealth, global power, and myths of prosperity for all have produced spiritual and cognitive grief, alienation, and hopelessness that is personal and communal. Christopher Lasch writes about the devastation of personal life in the United States. He observes the "void within," the shutting down of feelings and underlying desperation and resignation prevalent among the middle classes and among the poor. He claims that experiences of emptiness, loneliness, and inauthenticity arise from the warlike conditions of American society, "the war of all against all" (Lasch 21-26).

In a similar vein, African-American culture critics trace the shape of despair in their communities. Cornell West speaks of "nihilism" and the "murky waters of dread and despair that now flood the streets of black America . . . the monumental eclipse of hope, the unprecedented crisis of meaning, the incredible disregard for human (especially black) life and property" (West 19). Hooks shares West's analysis of African-American life when she tells of "life-threatening despair in the black community," of a legacy of unreconciled grief that has been the breeding ground for profound nihilistic despair. "Many people openly acknowledge that they are consumed by feelings of self-hatred, who feel worthless, who want a way out. Often they are too trapped by paralyzing despair to be able to engage effectively in any movement for social change" (hooks 1994, 246-247).

The contours of despair are amorphous, a form of "cultural brokenheartedness" that threatens individual and communal life in the richest country in the world. Culture critics see inner devastation, numbness of spirit, and lack of hope. They point to the impossibility of gathering forces toward the common good of the nation and the globe because concealed despair saps our capacity for action. They invite lamentation.

Social Mechanisms of Denial

The dominant culture in the United States reinforces family systems of denial and squelches passions for human wholeness and for a new sense of meaning and connection. Social mechanisms of denial are legion; here are some, briefly and perhaps simplistically sketched:

1. *Consumerism.* Consumerism is a narcotic that absorbs our resources and anesthetizes us from pain. We obsess about money. And the acquisition of things is our principal system of meaning; it expresses and establishes class divisions among us. We use purchasing as "retail therapy" to restore sagging spirits, overcome despair, and defeat boredom (Schor 158-160; hooks 2000, 47). It does not work because we cannot have mutual relationships with things.

2. *Escapism.* We deny pain by living vicariously through celebrities, sports, and talk shows as "extensions of ourselves" (Lasch 21-22). We encourage pseudo-therapeutic confession about shame-filled and broken lives in public outpourings that receive no caring reception.
3. *Addictions.* We escape our despair by addictions—drugs, alcohol, and that assumed antidote to depression, workaholism.
4. *Violence.* We often displace our rage and alienation by scapegoating others, both foreigners and fellow Americans. We often disregard the dignity of life because we have no regard for our own.

Our denial in its various forms means the loss of our spirit and the diminishment of our humanity. The cost of denial in the United States is huge, but the impact of our denial on other peoples is far greater. The perfidious consequence of hidden hopelessness is that the possessing peoples "perpetuate—and in their most powerful institutions foster!—the status quo of the two-thirds world" (Hall). Denial of our own pain blocks our capacity to perceive and take into our being the afflictions of others. With walls of denial firmly in place against collective and personal despair, we will surely continue to deny or trivialize the pain of others. To extend a gentle reception to the pain of others, we need familiar knowledge of our own grief, anger, and doubt.

Without knowledge of our own pain, and no matter our good intentions, we make objects of others. We treat them as we wish to be treated, not as they need and desire to be treated (Bennett). We determine what is good for them, not they. Or we callously disregard their suffering because it frightens us too much or because we do not perceive our connections to them. These dynamics appear in family life, friendships, and discipleship of mission and ministry. Lamentations beckons us to confront our despair for our own sake and for the sake of the world.

Denying Pain

Cancer survivor and ethicist Arthur Frank shows how denial interferes with our ability to accept the pain of others. In his studies of testimonies of people coping with catastrophic illness, he reports how difficult it can be for them to gain a hearing, particularly when the illness throws their lives into chaos. Such stories evoke "wrenching and terrifying experiences within the listener," calling forth both one's past sufferings and the "fear that the listener's own life is equally precarious and fragile" (Frank 98). Rather than face these anxieties, listeners in these situations and others often try to silence the speaker or to impose a happy ending upon the story.

Similar denial and consequent deafness to stories of profound suffering appear in interviews with Holocaust survivors. Lawrence Langer reports that interviewers of survivors were not able to listen to the rawness and brutality of their experiences: "They could not hear the *whole* story of the atrocity and the speakers' efforts to give words to their experiences." Instead, interviewers kept driving the testimonies toward "accounts of human resilience or liberation." They wanted to rush to hope and to what might have been gained in the suffering, turning testimony of pain "into spiritual odysseys leading to easy familiarity with their content" (Langer 1991, xiv; see also Frank 101).

Denial of pain is not uncommon among seminarians and theology students, and it impairs mission, ministry, and relationships among families and friends. Sometimes students begin their studies seeking to heal the world but fail to recognize their own brokenness as a source of that zeal. They discover needs of street people, the ill, or survivors of global tragedies without asking why they themselves are so drawn to the afflicted, or alternatively, why they want to work only with the healthy and the prosperous.

Overlooking intimate connections between their inner worlds and the plight of others, the students deprive themselves of one of their deepest resources of empathy and compassion. Without their own stories, ministry becomes a projection of their wounds onto the world, or mission becomes a one-way street in which the "whole" condescend to help the "broken." In these imbalanced relations, the afflicted become objects instead of subjects; the well-intentioned burn out; and solidarity, mutuality, and friendship are thwarted.

I am convinced that denial not of guilt but of pain contributes to the racial divide in the United States. When we cannot hear others' suffering and receive it without defensiveness or extreme fear, we perpetuate resentment and misunderstanding. James Cone puts it well. By trivializing or ignoring black suffering, by not providing sufficient space for the stories of past racial atrocities to emerge, the white community dishonors, trivializes, and violates the humanity of African Americans. To forget suffering, to "let bygones be bygones," is to forget the victim, and so the causes of present pain are never uncovered and confronted (in Copeland 123).

In a similar vein, Robert Schreiter tells of the necessity of overcoming denial and honoring voices of pain for political reconciliation to occur in countries recovering from the violence of totalitarian regimes, such as South Africa. In moving from repression and violence during processes of reconciliation, he argues:

A new world order cannot be made by simply ignoring or repressing the memory of the violent past. Not to remember what has happened will likely mean that we will end up inventing new ways of continuing that cycle of violence. (Schreiter 1)

Even churches can be guilty of denial and amnesia because they "operate with a model of harmony and cooperation and thereby ignore conflict, clashing interests, and past sufferings" (Schreiter 23). The truth, to the degree it can be known, is the condition for moving forward.

Denise Ackermann agrees that truth about pain and suffering is a precondition for reconciliation. "Accountability requires *awareness*," and the truth of the past must be spoken (Ackermann 50). She proposes that whites as well as victims of South African apartheid need to lament. Whites need to lament to heal "the wound that oppressors inflict on themselves." The act of lamenting can help overcome entrenched denial because it puts truth into the open and brings awareness in accumulating layers of that which has been denied. Chances that one will become aware, she claims, are "in direct proportion to the amount of truth you can take without running away." Lamenting "enables individuals and communities to break with the past without forgetting it," and so can be a public act of reconciliation (Ackermann 52, 51, 55).

Lamentations Denies Denial

The biblical book of Lamentations refuses denial, practices truth-telling, and reverses amnesia. It invites readers into pain, chaos, and brutality, both human and divine. It conveys effects of trauma, loss, and grief beyond tears. Because God's voice is absent, it gives primacy to suffering voices like no other biblical book.

Yet even as the voices in Lamentations speak in beautiful, ordered poetry, they assert the impossibility of fully articulating their suffering, for "is there any pain like my pain?" (1:12); it is "great as the sea" (2:13). "Memories of trauma—the loss of a loved one, the experience of betrayal, the violation of basic human rights—become centers of pain that paralyze everything around them" (Schreiter 1998, 45; see Lifton). Torture and genocide are beyond speech, as many survivors of the Holocaust rightly insist. But half a century later, literature by and about Holocaust survivors continues to burgeon. Although lamenting the truth in even a partial way can take generations, there is no way forward without bringing suffering to voice.

When we live with a world destroyed, when we find our lives evoked by the world of the speakers, Lamentations becomes a mirror of our sorrow, loss, and doubt. It creates a framework, a larger world to which individual and community suffering can be related. We are no longer alone in our suffering because it is called forth, acknowledged, and named, no matter how indirectly, no matter how veiled by the text's metaphors and images. Art that leaps across the centuries can mirror our lives, echo our circumstances, and validate our experience of divine absence. We are not the first to find no God seeing, no God hearing, no comforting presence to uphold us. We are not the first to long for the missing voice or to plead for God's attention and not receive it.

The voices of Lamentations urge readers to face suffering, to speak of it, to be dangerous proclaimers of the truths that nations, families, and individuals prefer to repress. They invite us to honor the pain muffled in our hearts, overlooked in our society, and crying for our attention in other parts of the world. In this way Lamentations can shelter the tears of the world.

Lamentations can do this because sorrow and her companions are alone in the house. They have the space to live and come to the center of life, to express themselves in the empty rooms and become visible. The first condition for healing is to bring the pain and suffering into view. Only then can they be examined, allowed, and given their due. Demand their due they will; they will neither diminish nor disappear until they are met face to face.

Pain kept from speech, pushed underground and denied, will turn and twist and tunnel like a ferret until it grows in those lightless spaces into a violent, unrecognizable monster. Whether in personal therapeutic or political terms, Lamentations invites us into healing by giving speech to pain. It offers us language, form, and the power of example.

Compassionate and just relations among peoples cannot happen without overcoming repression and denial, casting off "narratives of the lie" (Schreiter 29-40). To hear voices of suffering without massive distortion it is necessary also to hear the grief and rage within ourselves. Without knowledge of our own wounds, the abyss in the lives of others will terrify us and make compassion impossible. And if our personal pain needs no attention at present, Lamentations still calls us to heed the voices of suffering around us. It reminds us that wholeness and reconciliation—personal, national, and global—cannot occur without the articulation of suffering in the face of denial and injustice. It calls us to see.

8

Who Will Comfort You?

A Theology of Witness

Lamentations can shred the heart and spawn despair, but, paradoxically, by mirroring pain it can also comfort the afflicted and open the way toward healing. It can affirm the dignity of those who suffer, release their tears, and overcome their experience of abandonment. In this chapter I describe Lamentations' relentless search for comfort and the cries across the poems for someone to "see" the suffering of the people. I find in Lamentations the rudiments of a theology of witness with consequences for personal flourishing, for mission and ministry, and for political reconciliation.

After several years studying and teaching Lamentations, I keep asking myself why, of all the texts I study and teach, this one has captured me so thoroughly. There are professional answers, of course: the beauty of acrostic poetry, the power of dramatic voices, the exquisite density of language and imagery, the open-ended theological probing. But when I am honest, the answer is autobiographical. Lamentations has helped me to claim my inner world and calls me outward to the sufferings of the world. In Zion's place of comfortlessness and abandonment, I recognize aspects of my life for which I had no words. Lamentations calls to a deep part of me that was frozen and cut off like the marble statue in a poem by Elizabeth Barrett Browning entitled "Grief."

> I tell you, hopeless grief is passionless;
> That only men incredulous of despair,
> Half-taught in anguish, through the midnight air
> Beat upward to God's throne in loud access
> Of shrieking and reproach. Full desertness,

In souls as countries, lieth silent-bare
Under the blanching, vertical eye-glare
Of the absolute Heavens. Deep-hearted man, express
Grief for thy Dead in silence like to death—
Most like a monumental statue set
In everlasting watch and moveless woe
Till itself crumble to the dust beneath.
Touch it; the marble eyelids are not wet:
If it could weep, it could arise and go.

If it is true that "hopeless grief is passionless," then Lamentations must be hopeful, for it is "passion-full." It seeks access to God through an excess of "shrieking and reproach." It lets loose tears and chips away at the hardened, marbled statue of the spirit. The Bible's most comfortless book opens the way to comfort.

She Has No One to Comfort Her

Daughter Zion's comfortlessness reverberates like a sorrowful antiphon across the first poem and lingers implicitly across the book on behalf of a whole people. First, the narrator proclaims it, "There is no one to comfort her among all her lovers" (1:2b, 9b). Then, Daughter Zion cries out, "For these things I weep . . . because my comforter is far from me, one who would turn my spirit" (1:16). The narrator reiterates it, "Zion spread out her hands; there is no one to comfort her" (1:17), and Zion takes it up again when she calls upon God, "There is no one to comfort me" (1:21a).

But what could possibly bring this city woman comfort when she is bereft of everyone and everything that gave her life? How can pain be overcome "when a whole community is struck by disaster" (Heim 129-169)? What is the comforter's role in Lamentations? What does it mean to be comforted?

The comforter in ancient Israel may have been an official who spoke kindly to the aggrieved and who led mourning rituals, such as tearing clothes, throwing dirt in the air, pulling the hair (Pham 13-36; Fitzgerald; but see Hillers 20; Re'emi 73-134). Conversely, communities, friends, or official mourning women (Jer 9:17-22; O'Connor 1998b) may have performed the rituals, rather than one official mourner. Whatever the comforter's historical counterpart, the comforter in Lamentations does more than offer gestures and words—he or she is an elusive poetic figure whose absence emphasizes Zion's suffering isolation.

For the narrator, the comforter symbolizes just about anyone who would be with Zion in her desolation. But Daughter Zion seeks more than the mere presence of others; she seeks someone who would "turn *(šûb)* her spirit" (1:16). The Hebrew verb connotes "conversion," "turning around," "changing direction." Daughter Zion is looking for someone to help her re-orient herself, to turn her life away from the trauma that has overtaken her being. She declares unequivocally what she needs from a comforter: some-one to see the truth of her destroyed world and to grasp the encroaching despair and anger in which she dwells. She needs a faithful and empathetic witness to her pain.

From her first words, Zion announces her needs to those with ears to hear: "YHWH, look at *(rā'āh)* my affliction" (1:9c). She repeats her demand more emphatically with two Hebrew verbs of seeing: "Look *(rā'āh)* and pay at-tention" *(nābaṭ,* 1:11c). When God does not respond, she begs for comfort from the passersby, using the same verbs (1:12). At the end of chapter one, she adds emphasis to her petition. "See *(rā'āh)*, YHWH, I am in anguish. . . . Hear how I am groaning" (1:20a, 21a). God should use eyes and ears to absorb her anguish and to comprehend her distress. "See *(rā'āh)*, YHWH, and pay attention *(nābaṭ)* to whom you are acting so severely" (2:20a).

Hopes for rescue, restoration, and material goods may hide behind Zion's demands, but she asks only for a witness—for God, for someone, anyone, even strangers passing by—to see, pay attention, hear, to look at her (Dobbs-Allsopp 1997, 56-58; Frymer-Kensky 38). Only a witness who understands her world can begin to comfort her, but God does not see her. By contrast to Zion, the narrator asks nothing from God, yet the purpose of his urgent advice to Daughter Zion pushes in the same direction. He tells her to throw a tantrum, make a fuss, weep, cry out, pour out her heart, do anything to get God to notice her (2:18-19). By bringing to bear all her sorrow, exerting all her capacities of entreaty and persuasion, she may still get God to see her.

For God to see pain matters to other speakers in the book as well. The strongman also positions himself to elicit God's attention—"My eyes pour out without stopping . . . until YHWH looks down from heaven and sees" (3:49-50). In his case God does see and hear (3:59-61). Whether as wishful thinking, past remembrance, or present experience, he believes that YHWH has heard his voice and seen his case, and, assured of a reception, he is enabled to ask for action in similar requests. "You have heard my voice; do not hide your ears to my breathing and my cry for help" (3:56); "You have seen *(rā'āh)* my deprivation of justice," now "judge my cause" (3:59); and "You have heard their insult" (3:61), now "pay attention *(nābaṭ)* to their sitting and their rising" (3:63). Because the strongman has been seen and heard, because he has a witness for his suffering, he is able to hope and to look toward the future.

The community asks for nothing in chapter 4 (4:1-22), yet for good or ill God's "seeing" still matters. When God stops paying attention *(nābaṭ)* to the priests, they face suffering and exile (4:16a). And when God "observes" enemy Edom with care *(pāqad)*, the sins of that nation will be exposed (4:22). God's seeing vigilance remains the hope of the people.

Petitions for God to see take up all of the community's speech in chapter 5. Their opening line states their agenda in emphatic terms, "Remember, YHWH, what has happened to us, pay attention *(nābaṭ)* and see *(rā'āh)* our shame" (5:1). Yet compared to the shrieks and tears of earlier speakers, this long list of terrors (5:2-18) seems a muted, half-hearted appeal, as if hope of divine seeing were barely thinkable. If only God would see that their lives hang by a thread, that the old and the young dwindle and die, that desolation lies upon Zion like a smothering cloud (Gottlieb 71). But God does not see; the "cataract eyes of God" (Williams) may never see.

The Narrator Sees

The narrator alone sees Zion's suffering in its untamable immensity; he alone comprehends her desolation and loss. Whether officially or informally, he acts as her comforter and her witness. He is the one who pays her close attention, hears her, speaks kind words to her, and enters her world. But his encounter with her also changes him. No longer a dispassionate outsider to her sorrows, he becomes her impassioned advocate. Growing into the role of comforter, he does what God fails to do: he pays attention and his own spirit "turns" (2:1-19).

Zion's suffering makes claims upon the narrator and "turns his spirit." He has heard her charges against God in chapter 1, and his harsh accusations against her evaporate in another interpretation of her suffering. Now he stops blaming her and instead lashes out against her divine attacker. He accuses God of callous disregard and declares God out of control, not Zion. God has "become like an enemy" (2:5a), "killed all that was desirable to the eye" (2:4c), and "planned to destroy the walls of Daughter Zion" (2:8a). The narrator is an altered person in the world of this poetry.

Because the narrator sees the enormity of her pain, he is her comforter and her witness. His distance from her dissolves as his whole being responds to her suffering: "My eyes waste with tears; my bowels are in ferment; my bile is poured out on the ground because of the breaking of the daughter of my people" (2:11a, b). Linafelt insists that it is the plight of the children that prompts the narrator to sympathy (2:11c, 12), but it is Zion to whom he speaks (2000, 49-61). By seeing her and telling her what he sees, he acts as her witness. Even his comparison of her suffering to the sea mirrors back to her the depth of her desolation and conveys his empathy.

When the narrator attacks God, he speaks to readers and talks about God in the third person. Zion is the only figure whom he addresses in the book: "What can I say for you? What can I compare to you, O Daughter of Jerusalem?" (2:13). By speaking to her directly, he humanizes her, for she becomes a subject rather than an object to him. He treats her as a person, an agent, no longer merely the pitiable victim in a report. And he asks questions of her because she can tell him how to see her reality, how to be of help to her.

His questions mirror her pain as he tries to compare her suffering with something else, with some known and familiar loss (2:13). In the previous chapter she too sought a point of comparison and found none. "Is there any pain like my pain?" she asks (1:12b). Like her, the narrator looks for a comparison to her suffering, but finally nothing will suit. "Great as the sea is your breaking" (2:13c).

Even as the narrator compares Zion's suffering to the sea, he fails to contain it, to put boundaries around it and draw it into the visible distance. And because his comparison fails to reduce her pain to something manageable, he comforts her. He avoids inadequate or insulting comparisons that would reduce and falsify her pain, for it is "great as the sea," vast and overwhelming. And like the sea, its currents and tides reach unfathomable depths. "Who can heal you?" he asks. "No one" must be the answer. Because he sees her reality from her viewpoint and comprehends the unbounded sorrow she faces, he is her missing comforter. He has become her witness. Even as God refuses to take the role of witness in Lamentations, Zion gains a witness.

In Lamentations the afflicted need a comforting witness, neither the evangelist who announces messages from outside suffering nor the legal witness in a court of law who "objectively" states the facts, but something at once simpler and more difficult. The witness sees suffering for what it is, without denying it, twisting it into a story of endurance, or giving it a happy ending. The witness has a profound and rare human capacity to give reverent attention to sufferers and reflect their truth back to them. And in the encounter with those who suffer, the witness undergoes conversion from numbed or removed observer to passionate advocate.

In Lamentations the narrator sees and hears the magnitude of Zion's suffering (chap. 2). He does not deny it, reduce it to a nicer version of itself, or blanket it with theological platitudes. Instead, he reflects back to her the pain she can barely articulate. And somehow, his ability to admit her reality into his consciousness changes him; his encounter with her "turns his spirit" (cf. 1:16b). He grasps the truth about her situation and affirms that her suffering overwhelms him as well.

You Have to Come Close

In the aftermath of the death of his nineteen-year-old son, Eric, in a mountain-climbing accident, Nicholas Wolterstorff tells how he needed a comforter to see the enormity of his pain:

> But please: Don't say it's not really so bad. Because it is. Death is awful, demonic. If you think your task as comforter is to tell me that really, all things considered, it's not so bad, you do not sit with me in my grief but place yourself off in the distance away from me. Over there, you are of no help. What I need to hear from you is that you recognize how painful it is. I need to hear from you that you are with me in my desperation. To comfort me, you have to come close. Come sit beside me on my mourning bench. (Wolterstorff 34)

Like the speakers in Lamentations, Wolterstorff requires that his comforter see, pay attention to, and recognize the depth of his loss. He searches for someone who can enter his world, and if a witness could understand how painful it is, this bereft father might rejoin community, if only fleetingly.

The narrator's tears, his bodily turmoil, and his listing of Zion's sorrows, losses, and her shaming abandonment reveal how his encounter with her has shaken him from his marbled numbness. Although he is powerless to act on her behalf, he has enormous power to stand and let her pain address him. He sees that what has befallen her is unspeakable. He sees her truth and this is how he comforts her. In that reverent attention she is no longer alone with her catastrophe. His seeing is the indispensable event that invites her back into human connection.

But how does a witness bring comfort and release? Why can "being seen" liberate and open a way toward healing? The potential effects of gaining a witness, of having someone see and pay attention, are many. Elaine Scarry (35) writes that intense physical pain silences speech; overwhelming suffering is language-destroying. Physical pain is unsharable because it attacks both dignity and identity and so its force destroys speech.

If pain is a silencer of words and a destroyer of self (Walton), then the witness's acts of seeing and speaking of harm done give language back. The person or the community begins to make pain sharable by naming it and thereby create a space for sufferers to regain connections with themselves.

And in turn, being seen helps those who suffer regain human dignity because it affirms their experiences of pain. It enables them to emerge from isolation because they have made a human connection outside themselves.

Being seen restores those who suffer to community. Psychotherapist Judith Herman studies survivors of trauma from child abuse to captivity and warfare. Like Scarry on physical pain, Herman observes that psychological pain from trauma renders victims powerless and isolates them from human connection. To recover, victims must regain power and reestablish relationships. The witness who receives the pain breaks that isolation and creates a sacred bond with sufferers that at first simply accompanies them, and then this renews their dignity and enables them slowly to regain identity.

Mirroring Pain

Acknowledging and reflecting back suffering restores the humanity of victims because it validates their perception of the way the world has fallen away from under their feet. Bell hooks's account of a conversation with her mother depicts the liberating effect of gaining a witness.

> One day I called my mother. "Daddy didn't love me." "Of course he loved you, he did this and this." But this time after hours of torturous conversation, she suddenly said, "You're right—he didn't love you" . . . and the moment of her acknowledging the truth of what I had experienced was such a moment of relief! The moment she affirmed the reality of what had taken place, I was *released* because somehow . . . it's the act of *living the fiction* that produces the tortuous angst and the anguish . . . the feeling that you're mindfucked. (hooks 2000, 222)

Hooks's mother released her from living with a lie she could not overcome alone. By confirming hooks's version of childhood events, her mother gave her back herself, and she was no longer isolated in her pain. Healing could begin because she had a witness.

Robert Schreiter writes about similar dynamics in the painstaking process of reconciliation within societies emerging from military and political violence. Before any movement beyond factional hatred and desire for vengeance can even begin, victims of violence need to be received by compassionate others. They need to be seen and heard.

> Attention . . . is the basis of compassion, of an ability to be with, to walk alongside victims at the victim's pace. The root of the word

compassion is, of course, "to feel or suffer with." We can never entirely enter into another's suffering, although we can enter again our own suffering, which might parallel that of another. What we may lack in empathy or parallel experience we can make up in attention, an attention that does not impale the victim but creates an environment of trust and safety. (Schreiter 72-73)

Reverent attention by witnesses creates trust and safety necessary to retrieve and heal painful memories. For Schreiter, this attention is the "essence of reconciliation" (72). Witnesses enable people to tell what happened to them, a telling that must occur over and over. In the repeated telling and reception of stories, survivors reenter the experience, relive it emotionally, and may thereby be able to come to grips with what happened to them. When the truth finally comes out, they overcome the state's version of truth, the "narrative of the lie," and expose it in its full venom. Only such a process can break the violent, looping chain of revenge and restore humanity to victims and perpetrators alike. Then healing may begin.

Poetry as Salvation

As the narrator is to Zion, so the book can be to readers—a comforting witness. Lamentations creates a world, a poetic space outside life, akin to readers' own worlds. The book's ancient audience—survivors of either Jerusalem's fall to the Babylonians or some other invasion of the city— would find in it a reflection of their destroyed lives, although in poetic rather than precise historical terms. And Lamentations' poetic artistry gives it the capacity to mirror pain across the ages. Precisely because its own terrain is so dismal, the book is a "seeing" that gives language and imagery to the silenced or barely glimpsed pain of its readers. In the intricate artistry and emotive force of its poetic world, survivors see what they already know. Their old world is over, the God they knew is gone, their suffering is beyond compare. Even if the book's subject is "nostalgia, despair, frustration, it still creates a form of salvation" (Camus 263n.).

The poetry of Lamentations is a way of working through death, though new life may be nowhere on the horizon. As Jane Cooper says about poetry in general, Lamentations is a form of "survival that keeps revealing itself as an art of the unexpected" (122). As literature of survival, it gives words and shape to inchoate and unspeakable experiences; it provides suffering's "necessary echo" from outside the experience (Gaughan), and it reveals survivors' fierce graspings for life in ways readers recognize to be true. Lamentations is an echo chamber and a hall of mirrors. Its reflections and sounds need not be literal or mimic the readers' worlds for them to find themselves in the world of the text. As a comforting witness Lamentations does what God fails to do. By honoring suffering, it may even wring tears from hardened marble statues and enable them "to arise and go."

A Theology of Witness

In many other biblical texts, especially Second Isaiah, God is the comforting witness (see the Epilogue herein), but not here, not yet, not in Lamentations. The book expresses a yearning, ferocious and unrealized, for such a God, but God's failure to fill the role sets it in relief and sharpens the needs of the book's poetic figures to find a witness. The dynamic of the comforting witness I have teased from Lamentations reverberates in personal and social realms and has ramifications for spirituality, for the work of justice and reconciliation, and for lives of ministry and discipleship. Based on yearning for divine action, Lamentations shows us how to relate to ourselves and one another.

The seeing, hearing, and comprehending by the witness must have the quality of attention that does not "impale the victim" (Schreiter 73). There are many ways to impale sufferers—our kin, our friends, our neighbors—with our good intentions. We can take over the victim's story, reinterpret it, impose theological categories on it, or by comparing it to other suffering, diminish it, warp it, or violate it. Anything that trivializes and belittles suffering impales the victim. Comforting witnesses allow the truth to emerge on its own terms in a spirit of patience; they refrain from interpreting others' realities for them, imposing theological visions upon them, or creating versions of their story that violate the reality (Walton 41-48). These actions indicate a failure of seeing.

Comparing suffering often trivializes pain and denies suffering. In Lamentations the narrator tries to comfort Zion with a comparison because an adequate comparison could set boundaries on her pain and enable her to see fragments of her experience in some other person, event, or city. It could help her to name it at some removed level. To imagine a suffering outside herself might help her endure it, so that her pain might seem human in scope, enough externalized that she could imagine surviving it. Because the narrator does not find an adequate comparison, he succeeds in affirming the magnitude of her suffering. He sees that it is unspeakable.

Comparing suffering fails to comfort because suffering is ultimately a spiritual phenomenon. Suffering opens a window on a limitless horizon that defies fences, borders, and walls. Daughter Zion recognizes this herself and refuses comparisons: "Is there any pain like my pain?" she cries (1:12b).

Her claim to superlative sorrow at first seems melodramatic and self-pity-ing in the extreme, but it is neither. Rather, it is a symbolic and spiritual confession. It expresses how elusive are the edges of her pain, how high and deep it goes, and how impossible it is to absorb and cope with it. No more pain can be heaped upon her; death would be a release (Mintz 3).

An article by E. Schlosser in the *Atlantic Monthly* entitled "A Grief Like No Other" uses similar language of unsurpassable suffering. The article tells of the grief of parents whose children have been murdered. "Grief like no other" makes neither an ontological nor a mathematical claim. It asserts in poetic language that this suffering is immeasurable and impossible to grasp, ameliorate, or perhaps even let into the mind. It does not matter that in other parts of the world more horrible things are happening to other people. Grief like no other means, simply, this grief cannot be borne.

When survivors of the Holocaust speak of the incomparability of those events, its uniqueness among other genocides, they insist like Daughter Zion that comparing sufferings trivializes them. Elie Wiesel, for example, claims that the Holocaust "transcends history" and calls it the "ultimate mystery, never to be comprehended or transmitted" (Roth and Berenbaum 3). The calculated planning and utter dehumanization of one people by another appears unmatched in human history.

Yet some African Americans counter that theirs is the most extreme suf-fering in human history. In an article with the evocative title, "Laying Claim to Sorrow beyond Words," Samuel G. Freedman reports claims of African Americans to longer, more devastating, and dehumanizing suffering. And who can argue that the slave trade, forced labor, the dehumanization of a racial group for centuries, and the continuing social and spiritual devasta-tions in its aftermath cannot claim at least equivalent horror? In the words of student Malik Zulu Shabazz, "The Black Holocaust is absolutely 100 times worse than the Jewish Holocaust or any other holocaust that's ever existed on the Earth. We not only have a holocaust; we've paid a hell of a cost. We've lost over 200 billion lives. Don't step in here with that six mil-lion" (Freedman A13).

We mishear claims of historical uniqueness if we limit their meaning to the literal, because such language is poetic and spiritual in import. Both the Holocaust and the long history of enslavement of black peoples are unbear-able in conception, execution, and impact. Period. Neither can be fully grasped nor even communicated in a way that does justice to the experi-ences of the people. The symbolic power of claims to uniqueness is far more important than any measuring intentions. Gerald Early asserts that "many black people feel that whites don't understand just how great an atrocity slavery was" (Freedman A13). Some African Americans adopt holocaust language to enable whites and themselves "to understand what slavery was and what it means" (Freedman A13).

Both the Holocaust and slavery in the Americas are beyond measure, beyond comparison. "Great as the sea" is the shattering of these people, and of the Palestinians, the Afghans, and the Rwandans. Profound suffering can never be measured. It escapes every effort to tame it and constrain it, at least for a very long time. Until others can see, hear, and receive survivors' testimonies, social conflict among "identity" groups will replicate itself. Racial harmony will remain elusive until we can see, hear, and pay attention to the pain of the other.

Jon Sobrino, a Spanish theologian working in El Salvador, himself a target of death squads, warned against comparing and measuring sufferings. At a lecture in the 1980s, Sobrino would not allow a comparison of the sufferings of middle-class Americans with the tragic pain of the people of El Salvador in the midst of civil war. Sobrino said quietly, "All suffering is sacred." He did not say that all suffering is equal, nor did he deny that some suffering arises from seemingly trivial losses and discomforts, nor that social violence and poverty compound ordinary human suffering in hugely disproportionate ways. Instead, he insisted that we cannot compare sufferings as if there were a competition among sorrows.

Sobrino acted as a witness to his North American audience; he saw that even people in the world's wealthiest country know tribulation and loss. He did not dismiss them as light or insignificant compared to the wrenching pain and death in his own country, nor did he trivialize their reality in order to insist on his own. His statement invited his listeners to attend to their own suffering, to face it, and to meet it with gentle compassion. When I reflect back on those words spoken in the 1980s, I see them as a great act of mercy. Sobrino's words comforted his listeners because we no longer had to assert our pain or block out stories of others' pain to protect ourselves from further emotional overload. That all suffering is sacred means that loss, dehumanization, and assaults on bodies and spirits of entire peoples or one tiny child must be seen and taken in somehow before being left behind.

Comparison of sufferings prevents seeing and denies truth. It imports language from outside that misnames the suffering at hand. One of my students judged the sudden collapse of a twenty-year marriage as a light thing to bear compared to atrocities in other parts of the world or to the suffering of Atlanta's homeless. The claim that her broken marriage was "nothing compared to . . . " might have come from confidence that she would survive this shock and grief, that she would rebuild her life. On the face of it, however, her comparison denied her true reality, that her own world had tumbled down around her in deeply hurtful ways. She could not minister to others because she was not a comforting witness to herself.

The comforting witness returns the sufferers to themselves, recognizes their dignity, and restores them to human community. Often these deeds of love and restoration are done quietly among family and friends, in the churches, and in towns and villages. Sometimes they are done in spiritual direction, counseling, and psychotherapy, and in national and international structures of reconciliation. Sometimes they are not done at all, and personal and communal cycles of grief, rage, and violence repeat themselves with escalating fury down through generations.

Rudiments of a theology of witness emerge from this study. The comforting witness of Lamentations suggests a way of being in the world that overcomes the dualism between inner life and involvement in the world. Lamentations' call to honor pain is not an invitation to solipsism, narcissism, or egocentric foolishness. To honor our own pain means to see it, to stop denying it, or comparing it, or trivializing it. It means to enter it as fully and squarely as we can, often in a long spiritual process. To do so is ultimately empowering and enables genuine love and action for others. It leads to the recognition that the domain of the self and the domain of the world flow into and out of each other. Discounting our own pain is a sure sign that we cannot be a reverent witness to the pain of others. To become witnesses requires that we be comforted, be witnessed, and ultimately become our own witnesses who treat with loving and gentle awareness the brokenness within.

The narrator was able to let Zion speak harsh and awful words. He heard her truth, saw her pain, and that communication, that glimpse of her broken world, changes him from her scathing critic to her passionate ally. He stops impaling her with his theology of blame and retribution. This ability to be open to others depends to some extent upon openness to self, but the process is not sequential. It is not first attend to your own wounds and then the wounds of the world. Contact with the suffering city woman changes the narrator and forces him to find resources within to look at her, though the text has no interest in his emotional life.

Yet the text implies that the suffering, afflicted, and broken have a gift for the witnesses, the gift of their own humanity. They call to us not for solutions but to be seen and embraced in their wounds, and in the process, they show us our own need of healing. "The victim asks the bystander to share the burden of the pain" (Chastain 173). But witnesses cannot share that burden when they are not aware of their own pain. The others' burdens will terrify them, blindside them, or drive them away. The wounds of the victims will evoke the witnesses' hidden closet of terrors.

Implied in Lamentations' dynamic of the comforting witness is a spirituality of attentiveness not merely to the beauty, possibility, and wonder of creation but to internal conditions and external realities that deny the world's beauty, dehumanize others, and diminish life on this earth. Although Lamentations never denies human sin, mirroring back that sin is only a marginal concern of the book. Instead, it faces us with our despairing, deadened beings and calls us to honor the voices of pain, loss, anger, and resistance in ourselves and around us. To be witnesses to the suffering of others requires the gathering up of our passions, something that cannot be done by willpower alone. Only as our spirits find release from numbness, from their marbled protections, and from their passion-quenching denial can we relate to others in solidarity and compassion that does not make them objects of our own needs.

Failing to find a comforting witness in childhood or adulthood, our lives may languish; failing to know when we need one, our spirits may wobble in uncertainty. Even well-intentioned believers may not find energy and resolve to praise God with all their strength, to work for justice, and to resist dehumanization of others. Instead, we diffuse our strength; mission, ministry, and simple caring become barren enterprises performed out of duty or not performed at all. Lamentations calls us to a conversion of ourselves toward ourselves so that we can turn to God and others. It invites a seeing of the anxiety, despair, and the apathy that prevent us from knowing our connections with others.

Despair Work

Joanna Macy writes that the United States ignores despair and anxiety because of social taboos. Even religious communities overlook despair because to express it appears as a lack of faith. The refusal to acknowledge despair produces emotional and sensory deprivation, psychic numbing, and impedes our capacity fully to respond to others. Its cause, Macy argues, is not mere indifference but the fear of confronting despair that "lurks subliminally beneath the tenor of life-as-usual" (Macy 15).

She urges us to do "despair work," because despair cannot be banished by simple injections of optimism or sermons on "positive thinking." To feel despair in this cultural setting is isolating, but it may well be a healthy response to ecological and social perils that threaten the globe. And she reminds us that in the spirit of Christian and Buddhist contemplatives, falling apart is not necessarily a bad thing. It may break down the wall of silence, open new worlds, and create new possibilities. Confrontation with despair does not bring loneliness and isolation but renewed life and truer community (Macy 16-28).

Lamentations summons us to our despair, personal and cultural. In honoring Zion's pain it invites us to be truthful about our own, or at least not to discount it as unimportant. It invites us to feel, to permit ourselves to feel, and to find images for sorrow and loss that rise from hidden graves within. To be comforting witnesses, sooner or later, we must face our own pain; there is no other way. Though an arduous process for some, the facing of pain is liberation, release, grace, redemption.

It is also true that communities and individuals who have known death squads, torture, and dehumanizing abuse cannot speak of healing or comfort until they are ready. "Time doesn't heal all wounds," writes Charlie Walton, who lost two sons in an automobile accident. Even years after, he writes, "I experience the full force of the emotional hurricane over and over again . . . but with longer periods of quiet in between" (Walton 91). Some survivors of the Holocaust believe that to talk of comfort or of moving forward obscenely trivializes the overwhelming horror, dehumanization, and destruction in the calculated evil of attempted genocide; this is surely true. But it also shows the devastation wrought by the Holocaust, which not only tried to destroy the life of a people but also put Western culture and Jewish and Christian theologies in grave doubt.

Missioners in Cambodia, for instance, describe the statue-like numbness of the people, old and young alike, in the wake of the "killing fields" (L. Arens, M.M., personal communication 1998; J. Quinn, M.M., personal communication 1993). It may take generations to be able to revisit the past in even the most superficial manner, and they may never be ready to do so. Still, the process of regaining humanity and coming even to the threshold of human flourishing requires engagement with that past in all its evil, betrayal, and pain.

The call to conversion I find in Lamentations' portrait of the narrator is important for this society. The narrator is changed by seeing and hearing and attending to the pain of Zion. He listens to her testimony and that alters the way he sees the world and God. His conversion results from being able to let her unspeakable reality into his being. When he does that, everything changes.

9

The Abusing God

Although God never speaks directly in Lamentations, the book is highly theological. Four of its five poems speak to God, and all five have something to say about God. The speakers rarely attempt to appease God, and they do not spare God. Although they offer contradictory testimonies, the predominant opinion among them is that God is cruel and violently abusive.

Lamentations' speech about an absent, abusing God is a blessing, an unnerving but refreshing iconoclasm. It smashes images of a God harnessed to our bidding. It disrupts theologies of a God who makes us prosper in all things, rescues us from every evil, and longs always to be with us. By insisting on honest testimony from the midst of pain, the book takes us to that place of impasse that purges and burns away pseudo-spiritualities and God-diminishing pieties. It invites us into vulnerability where God can be met in what Christians call the Paschal Mystery.

Yet even if the book liberates God from "yes" theologies and opens us to a new experience of God in the midst of a "no," how can we live with its speech? Is this reliable theology? Does it witness to God's own being? These questions impinge directly upon my faith, for if God is abusive and violent toward the wicked and innocent alike, then I resist and refuse. I withdraw my allegiance. Such a God is simply not acceptable (Joyce 1993, 319).

If God abuses and cruelly and violently controls us, then it is surely fine for humans to be abusive and violently controlling as well. The ways we imagine God encourage, support, and affirm our own behavior. An abusing God leaves abuse and violence unchallenged in families, churches, and nations. If God is abusive, then God is unjust and immoral. If God is abusive, victims of abuse are without refuge, tyrants and bullies cannot be restrained, and love can never be trusted.

God's Character

In Lamentations, God's character emerges from the testimonies of speakers, not from God's direct appearances, for there are none. In a chorus of contradictions, poetic voices tell of God's deeds and motivations in regard to the people's suffering. This chapter studies the character of God in Lamentations, first by surveying the speakers' testimonies, then by examining some contemporary approaches to God's violent character, and finally by offering my own uneasy theological compromises.

When speakers interpret Zion's suffering as punishment for her sins, they are reiterating an ethical vision solidly affirmed in their inherited traditions. Deuteronomistic and prophetic writers understood loss of the land as punishment for sin (Gottwald 1954, 66-71; Albrektson 231-237). In Lamentations, nation and city have already fallen, overwhelming suffering is the present predicament, and prophetic theology is ready to explain. Such is the narrator's starting point: "YHWH has caused her suffering for her many transgressions" (1:5b).

According to this view, God's punishment of Jerusalem is an act of justice, and God is neither whimsical nor cruel in administering it. But even as speakers in Lamentations name Zion's suffering as well-deserved punishment, they also declare God to be whimsical and cruelly fickle (Dobbs-Allsopp 1997, 45-54). Testimony about God's justice and God's cruel abusiveness creates a kind of counterpoint in Lamentations. Speakers move back and forth in defending and berating God for the city's suffering. God's character remains unresolved, unsettled, and open ended, but the larger share of testimony bewails God's unreliability and abusiveness.

Zion begins to speak as if God were receptive to communication with her (1:9c, 11c), but then her view changes abruptly. She tells of divine assault upon her and undermines the narrator's ethical vision of God's character (Dobbs-Allsopp 1997, 47-48). YHWH inflicts pain, sends fire into her bones, spreads a net for her feet, turns her back, leaves her devastated and faint, ties her sins around her neck in a yoke, gives her over to her enemies' hands. God treads upon her like grapes in a winepress (1:12c-15). The mere accumulation of violent deeds here and elsewhere implies that, if this is punishment, it exceeds all bounds, all proportionality to the sin. The God who should protect and cherish her has battered and harmed her in every way short of killing her.

Still the vision of a just, punishing God reemerges in her speech. She excuses God and blames herself, like a battered spouse returning to her abuser. She rebelled; she provoked; she took lovers; she deserves punishment (1:18-19). But something is amiss, she implies, because God does not distribute punishment fairly. "Let all their wickedness come before you and deal severely with them as you have dealt severely with me" (1:22b, a). Although Zion does not entirely reject her inherited theology, it begins to crumble under her charges.

The narrator learns from her and alters his own view of God's character. What drives God is abusive rage, not justice. "How Adonai in his anger has set Daughter Zion under a cloud" (2:1). A whirling storm of harsh verbs relates God's unbridled fury against Zion: God cast down, did not remember, swallowed up, did not spare, threw down, brought down to the ground, hewed down, burned against, bent his bow, killed all, poured out rage, became an enemy, ruined, tore down, destroyed, spurned, rejected, abhorred, planned to destroy, shattered (2:1-9). God's acts appear indefensible. Even if Zion is guilty, it no longer matters.

Across this violent outbreak the narrator steadily decries God's anger. It burns, rages like fire, an indignant force that consumes, overthrows, and shatters its object (2:1a, b, 2b, 3a, 4c, 6c). Even if this is punishment for sin, God's administration of it is out of control. Worse still, this outrageous destructiveness was premeditated, announced in advance. "YHWH did what he planned. He accomplished his word that he commanded from days of old" (2:17). God is in the wrong now, not she. God is on trial.

Despite God's punishing violence, the narrator advises Zion to cast herself upon divine mercy. Despite his bitter indictments, he relies on God's willingness to be stirred by the city woman's plight. "Pour out your heart like water before the face of Adonai" (2:19). With waterfalls of tears she should draw God's attention to herself, but God does not reply.

When Zion speaks, she appears to have gained strength from the narrator and, with a heightened fury of her own, she implores God to see the consequences of divine anger (2:20-22). Women eat their children, and priests and prophets, young and old are dead. "You killed them on the day of your anger; you slaughtered; you did not pity" (2:21). "You summoned" the enemies; no one escaped or survived; the little ones I bore and reared, you destroyed. It was the day of your anger (2:21, 22). God is more than unreliable; God is a heartless murderer.

The strongman's view of the divine character is the most contradictory in the book. At one moment he makes God his bitter assailant and the next his rescuer of countless mercies. Images of assault pile upon one another in deadening tumult in his testimony. The unnamed opponent who captures and attacks him (3:1-19) turns out to be God (3:31-33, 37-38). God drives him into darkness, causes his flesh and skin to waste, breaks his bones, surrounds him with wormwood and weariness, treats him as if he were dead, walls him in, shuts out his prayer, twists his path (3:1-19). Like a wild beast, God attacks him, tears him to pieces, makes him desolate, shoots arrows at him, fills him with bitterness, saturates him with poisonous worm-wood, crushes his teeth with gravel, and makes him cower in the dust. God is his torturer.

But suddenly, in the pattern typical of the lament form, the speaker re-verts to hope. He remembers something of God's character that evokes trust.

> The steadfast love of YHWH is not finished, for his mercies do not come to an end. They are new every morning. Great is your faith-fulness. "YHWH is my portion," says my soul; therefore I hope in him. (3:22)

God's true character abounds in love, mercy, and faithfulness. Despite the strongman's experience of God as a torturer, he will not relinquish hope in a God of covenant loyalty. Does the strongman think God has good rea-sons for the attacks, or is he holding stubbornly, desperately to past mean-ing and past confidence despite debilitating realities?

The Dilemma

For ancient peoples as well as many contemporary ones, God causes ev-erything that happens, both good and bad. Disaster and well-being both flow from God, who "causes grief but has mercy according to the greatness of his steadfast love" (3:32). For the strongman, there is no exit from the contradiction that both good and bad originate in God's being. Events origi-nate in God's will, in the world of the spirits, in the heavenly realm, not in chaotic historical forces or natural events. The heart of the book's theologi-cal problem is the view that God comes in grace and mercy and the same God also batters, assaults, and punishes. Suffering must be divine punish-ment for sin in this view, for arbitrary suffering would imply an arbitrary God. If God is all-powerful and just, then everything that hurts, dehuman-izes, and destroys must arise from human failure. Lamentations struggles mightily to keep both divine power and justice intact.

Yet in a comment about God's motivation (3:33), the strongman hints at a tantalizing alternative view of God's character. The verse is noticeable not only for its place in the middle of the chapter, but because it changes the divine name to the title Adonai ("my Lord"), drawing further attention to itself. Smack in the middle of this highly structured, sixty-six line acrostic, the speaker asserts, "He [Adonai] does not afflict willingly nor grieve the children of humans" (3:33). This line is startling and means literally that God does not afflict or grieve "from his heart" *(millibbô).*

Somehow, the strongman implies, God does not want to grieve and afflict. God is not wholehearted in these punishing, abusive attacks. God is unwilling, inwardly divided, and struggling over works of punishing anger. Perhaps God is under constraint from outside sources, principles, or laws that govern the world. Perhaps God does not have direct power to intervene against chaotic forces of history, human decisions, or natural events.

The proposal that God is in some way powerless over human evil suggests another way to think of God's character. Perhaps God's power takes a form other than that of controlling domination as God struggles, suffers, and resists evil. Lamentations does not say this, of course, but divine unwillingness to grieve and afflict, placed in the book's exact center, opens a small crack in a theological prison onto vast mystery.

But as if a vulnerable God were impossible even to imagine, the strongman pulls back to the familiar world of an all-powerful deity of hierarchical relations. "Who can speak and it happens, if Adonai does not command?" (3:37). "Do not the good and the bad both go out from the mouth of the Most High?" (3:38). Since God is all-powerful and just, the people must have sinned, he concludes (3:40-42). "We have transgressed and rebelled" (3:42a). But their confession lacks the specifics to make it convincing. Should they not say more? Should they not name precise infractions of law, covenant, or relationship with God? (1:2, 8-9, 19; 4:13-15). The people's confession rings hollow, but their sins do not matter anymore to the strongman because God has not forgiven! (3:42). God kills viciously, pitilessly, and hides from them behind a cloud (3:42-45). God's character is not reliably forgiving; God has failed them.

But in yet another theological turn, the strongman throws himself upon God, weeping "until YHWH looks down from heaven and sees!" (3:50). He tries every tactic to persuade the blind, hiding God to desist from attack and see his plight. "From the bottom of the pit," he calls (3:55). Waters rise over him; a stone closes out light and life. He is about to die, but paradoxically the place of death is also the place of life. "You have heard my voice," he declares. "You have drawn near on the day I called you and have said, 'Do not fear'" (3:55-57).

Whether the strongman remembers a past encounter, experiences God anew, or engages in wishful thinking, he finds assurance and comfort in the pit, the bottom-most point in his lament. He finds a protector who pleads his cause, redeems his life, and "sees" the injustice (3:58-59). Even so, rescue is but a hope, for affliction and threat of annihilation still loom and enemies still mock (3:62-63).

At the poem's end, the strongman's perceptions of God differ sharply from the beginning. Without resolving his theological problem, he arrives at hope only after hope has vanished. Then hope appears unbidden in the thick of despair, not apart from it. Unresolved tension, enormous doubt, and intellectual confusion coexist with hope. Hope comes, fades, eludes, disappearing as if God has come into the room and left again. The strongman's theology is stuck in the problem of evil. Yet when he asserts that God does not afflict and grieve willingly (3:33), he chips away at images of an abusing God, if only for an instant.

Chapter 4 is the least theological in the book. The speaker is not hopeful but enervated, barely surviving under foreign occupation. "YHWH accomplished his wrath; he poured out his burning anger. He kindled a fire in Zion and it devoured her foundations" (4:11). God is a fire-setter, a destroying arsonist, provoked by the sin of religious leaders (4:13-16), and once again massive destruction is the fault of people. Yet the arsonist God, also disposed toward justice, will overturn enemy Edom for its iniquity (4:22). But that will be in the future. At present, Zion and her inhabitants barely subsist.

Despite the despair expressed so far in the book, in chapter 5 the community still hopes for reprieve from God. "Remember, YHWH, what has happened to us; pay attention and see our shame" (5:1), they plead. In the body of this chapter they make no charges against God but merely tell God about devastation in the city, which is now prowled by jackals (5:2-18). But in the final petition they demand to know why God has abandoned them. "Why have you forgotten us forever? Why have you abandoned us these many days? Return us to yourself, YHWH, and we will return; renew our days as of old" (5:20-21).

In the book's final lines there is no explanation of the catastrophe and its enduring tragedies except that God has rejected them. Human sinfulness cannot explain their suffering, only God's turning away. "Return us to yourself, YHWH, . . . unless you have utterly rejected us and you are angry with us forever" (5:22). Lamentations has no happy ending; the divine-human relationship is shattered, and God neglects, abuses, and rejects them, perhaps forever. God's abandonment of them ends the book (Dobbs-Allsopp 1993, 94; Linafelt 2001; Provan 134).

Lamentations' Portrait of God

The character of God in Lamentations is complex, even contradictory. The poetry juxtaposes the God of mercy and justice, who punishes sinners and rewards the faithful, with the God of cruelty and abuse, who inexplicably burns, kills, and abandons. It forces us to struggle with the contradictions, to resist easy theologies, and perhaps most beneficial, to honor the struggles of many in extreme suffering who also wonder if God has abandoned them forever.

These character contradictions of God in Lamentations and other biblical texts present immense difficulties for thoughtful believers. The blessings of the book's bracing iconoclasm notwithstanding, God's violent abuse undermines and makes utterly unreliable God's covenant love. Here are four approaches for reflecting on the problem of God's abusive character in Lamentations.

1. *The Ignore-Divine-Violence Approach.* A common, uncritical response to divine abusiveness in this and other biblical texts is simply to ignore it and choose instead to embrace only texts that portray a loving and merciful deity. Such an approach is reassuring and appealing and is close to the actual practice of the churches in their nearly exclusive use of words of hope in Lamentations 3. But this theological selectivity leaves people with only part of the biblical testimony. It ignores Lamentations' capacity to mirror tragic experiences of believers. It shrinks God to controllable proportions, dissolves God's freedom into "positive thinking," and eradicates human accountability from the divine-human relationship.

2. *The Justify-Divine-Violence Approach.* More commonly people justify God's violence and accept with surprising readiness the idea of a punishing God who causes pain in any extreme to make us malleable to God's will. God has no choice, even if unwilling (3:33), but to punish sinners. Like Job's friends, this approach defends God and heaps guilt on people. Job's friends propose that, knowingly or unknowingly, Job deserved the tragedies God brought upon him. Yet the book clearly rejects the friends' viewpoint in favor of Job's angry indictments of God (Job 42:8).

Justifiers of divine violence have some good points. Undeniably, we sometimes do bring suffering upon ourselves; we do sin by commission and omission before God and each other. But divine action against human sin is simply inadequate to explain suffering. In the aftermath of the Holocaust, killings in Cambodia, slaughter in Rwanda, and countless other catastrophes of recent history, and in view of scientific and historical understandings of causality, to blame God for all things in some literal way seems preposterous.

Alice Miller helps explain cultural predispositions to interpret suffering as divine punishment for human failure. In *Breaking Down the Wall of Silence* she finds in Lamentations—in words she credits to the prophet Jeremiah—the typical pattern of abusive relationships. The speaker takes blame on himself the way abused children take on guilt rather than blame their parents for neglect and cruelty. "He constantly tries to seek comfort in the thought that torture is not more than the just and necessary punishment for his own misdemeanors" (Miller 1991, 117).

Biblical scholars can find things to challenge in Miller's precritical interpretation. As a psychotherapist, however, Miller helps explain why so many people are ready to blame humans and excuse God. Abused children believe the opposite of their experiences of neglect and cruelty. Rather than accept the unbearable truth that their parents have betrayed them, they blame themselves; guilt becomes their only comfort! (Miller 1991, 23-24). In the abusive relationship, both parties justify violence as an expression of love "for your own good."

This pattern of relating extends easily from parents to other figures of authority and to God. But the common assumption that violence and abuse can be "a dimension of love" is false and dangerous. Violence and abuse in the name of love are not love but false love that masquerades as love. Physical or emotional violence "for the good of the other" can never be love (hooks 1999, 6).

Still, the afflicted and oppressed might claim a punishing God is a source of hope, for God will punish the high and the mighty and raise up the lowly. God alone ultimately balances the scales of justice, and only God can use violence for good ends. While such theology places a wedge between humans and violence—God alone uses violence—it leaves divine violence without criticism.

In Lamentations the problem of divine violence becomes particularly clear because God's punishing anger is directed at God's own people. Most poems in the book challenge the interpretation that human sin alone could have brought this enduring misery upon them. Divine punishment does not explain disaster.

3. *The Reject-Texts-about-the-Abusing-God Approach.* Some interpreters simply conclude that texts about God's abuse must be declared harmful and rejected. One proponent of this view holds that the Bible itself is suspect because the very notion of a monotheistic God is violent, teaches violence, and sets conditions for violence against others (Schwarz 5). Even as this approach rejects the Bible's unifying tendencies as exclusionary and inherently violent, it does set the issue clearly before us. God acts badly in Lamentations and other texts. The approach creates cautions about preaching and teaching unreflectively about a God who abuses, batters, and destroys. Because biblical texts are powerful artistic works and honored as sacred texts in communities of faith, they have great potential to sanction violence and abuse and, at the least, leave unchallenged the violence and abuse among us.

In the United States these texts are especially dangerous because this culture is saturated in violence (Williams 242). Indeed, founding myths of this country are violent, articulated over and over in the enduring image of the cowboy and his avatars, who employ violence in any extreme for the sake of the good. Yet results of our multifaceted and violent myth have been the subjugation and devastation of peoples and empty, dehumanized spirits of our own.

The declaration that some texts must be excluded from the canon, from liturgy, and from religious life, however, replicates the approach of the second-century heretic, Marcion, who declared the God of the Old Testament to be a God of judgment and violence and believed, therefore, that only the New Testament should be included in the canon. But only a few parts of the New Testament met his criteria of love and mercy, so he ended with a greatly reduced scripture. In 144 C.E., the church declared him a heretic and later insisted that the whole of both testaments were the scriptures of the church.

To excise the difficult texts erases possibilities of the texts to mirror present horrors, saves us from having to grapple with our own abuse and violence, and erases the cultural realities out of which the Bible emerged.

4. *God-Is-Both-Abusive-and-Loving Approach.* Walter Brueggemann (1997, 359-372) and David Blumenthal are among the few biblical interpreters who attempt to let the text's portrait of God as a violent abuser stand on its own terms. In vivid theological works both find unresolvable ambiguity in God's characterization, for God is both the One who comes in grace and mercy but also the One who abuses. God abuses, "but not all the time."

For Blumenthal, the faith claim that humans are made in God's image gives insight into God's behavior. Humans are undeniably violent and abusive, and if they are made in God's image, then God must be violent and abusive (Blumenthal 7-9, 7-19). For Brueggemann the biblical God is abusive, "on occasion" and "acts in ways not congruent with the claim . . . that Yahweh is 'steadfast and faithful'" (1997, 359). For both scholars, divine violence, anger, and abuse continue to endanger the world. Abusive anger and violence can break out at any time, because they are part of God's character.

Both Brueggemann and Blumenthal take the text's portrayal of divine character as strong testimony on the part of the Jewish community that God is free, sovereign, beyond human control. They hold fast to the awesome mystery, power, and freedom of the deity. They understand texts about God's abusiveness as fierce expressions of divine power, otherness, and transcendence. And they correctly insist that the biblical God really is sometimes violent and abusive. God is, for them, in Rudolph Otto's sense, a God to be feared, before whom to stand in awe, and also a fascinating and attracting God (Otto 63).

The obvious advantages of the God-is-both-abusive-and-loving approach is that the biblical testimony is left intact, and less appealing features of divine characterization are held in tension with those aspects of God's character that can be more easily embraced. This approach overcomes easy familiarity with God; it replaces either/or dualisms with both/and thinking; it seeks to balance God's transcendent otherness and grace-filled immanence; and it takes account of the whole canon.

But if Brueggemann and Blumenthal are right about God, if God really is violent and abusive as well as gracious and merciful, I want nothing to do with religion. If God's character is both abusive and merciful, as the biblical texts maintain, then there is nowhere for the abused to turn. There is no refuge in the storm, no way burdens can be lifted, no liberator from the violence humans have heaped upon each other from generation to generation. If this view is right about God, then God is unethical, and human ethics must be anchored elsewhere or abandoned altogether. God will never be trustworthy, for at any moment fiery anger can burst upon the world and destroy. Violent abuses of power in the world are inscribed within God and have their origins and model in God's own character. Violent oppression connects the heavens and the earth in a twisting Möbius strip of oppression.

Toward Another View

For years I have been struggling with the biblical character of God as violent and abusive, looking for a way that neither dismisses the biblical witness nor accepts it at face value. Here is my thinking so far.

The Bible is God's word, but it also reflects the culture that produced it. An enduring gain of historical-critical studies and, more recently, of postmodernism is the recognition that all texts, speech, and perspectives are culturally conditioned. That means, in part, that all texts, even sacred ones, arise from and are limited by historical circumstances. They participate in both the insights and the blindness of the communities that produce them. Some believe that the Bible escapes history and that as inspired word of God it contains universal messages equally suitable to all times and places. But that stance overlooks what Orlando Espín calls the "incarnational principle." God's word is embedded in, born into human culture. That is the way God decided to do it.

The Bible comes from a world vastly different from ours in language, forms, and ways of perceiving and acting in the world. It is a stranger, a cultural "other" among us (O'Connor 1998c, 329-330). Faith communities recognize this cultural gulf implicitly when they reject or ignore a panoply of biblical practices and laws. Christians, for example, do not follow dietary laws. Christians and Jews condemn slavery, treat rather than scorn lepers, permit divorce, do not pay bride prices, and fail to do any number of things the Bible commands.

Biblical language about God is as culturally conditioned as marriage customs and legal practices. When Lamentations speaks of God, it characterizes God in terms that made sense in its time and situation. Since Israel's ancient culture was based on relationships of honor and shame (Pilch and Malina 95-102), God must be a punishing and violent deity. In such a world, for human subordinates to betray God would require swift punishment because, according to their way of thinking, anything less would dishonor God. Moreover, ancient peoples understood the divine realm to be the direct source and origin of all things. They made no distinction between God's direct actions and chaotic events that occur in the world, so all things good and bad flow directly from God. The strongman is caught in just such a quandary. "Who can speak and it happens, if Adonai does not command?" (3:37).

But to hold that God orchestrates suffering in the world is obscene. God did not cause the Holocaust; kill students in school with guns; approve the destruction of Bosnia, Afghanistan, and Cambodia; cause clouds to withhold rain in Ethiopia; incite Hutus and Tutsis against each other in Rwanda; send the earthquakes in India and El Salvador; or cause the attacks on the World Trade Center and the Pentagon. The list goes on forever.

Historical and scientific thinking provides other ways to interpret catastrophe. Human evil, chance, chaos, the convergence of economic and social factors, greed, weather conditions—all converge in snowballing, whirling sets of complexities, failures, sinfulness, and unexpected consequences of human actions. God is not to blame except perhaps to the extent that God created a world in which forces and powers of good and evil coexist. Once set in motion, evil can overpower good, and the world returns to chaos (Jer 4:23-38).

Though I insist that we need Lamentations' bracing speech about God for its raw honesty and its iconoclastic power, in my view Lamentations' insistence on God's punishing violence must be critiqued for our time. It is wrong, because it insists on God's abusive power and violence as an aspect of divine freedom in the face of human pain. While Abraham Heschel rightly insisted that divine wrath reveals God to be passionately concerned with human life and human history, in Lamentations God's wrath exceeds all passion for justice and well-being. Erich Zenger asks, "Is it not high time that at least the great religions of humanity self-critically uncover *all* the violent perspectives in their own traditions, and move against them by a consistent nonviolence, especially in their official texts?" (Zenger 80).

So, then, have I joined with those who want to jettison abusive biblical texts? Tempting as that approach might be, it is too simple, naive, and costly. It throws away hints and glimmers of theological poetry that can bring us into new ways to imagine and to meet God. I propose, instead, that Lamentations' theological speech offers correcting and constructive possibilities.

Enter the Conversation

The first possibility is to recognize that biblical speech about God represents a multifaceted, polyphonic conversation already going on within Lamentations and within the Bible itself (Brueggemann 1997). The Bible is a conversation in process into which believers are invited from generation to generation. To the conversation we bring not only the biblical text but also our culture, our experiences, and our contemporary struggles and questions. Interpretation of biblical texts is always a conversation, not a one-way set of blueprints for life. That means that the biblical text is only one theological source in naming, approaching, and living with God. My Roman Catholic location becomes immediately evident when I take this stand.

But even those who profess *sola scriptura* (only the scriptures) include many for whom theology is "a rational wrestling with mystery" (McFarlane 1). Theologian Karl Barth held that scripture is not the word of God in itself but becomes the word of God in the context of community. The community must reincarnate the revealed word in its own context. This view opens the possibility of critical interaction with the text and is not far distant from the *Dogmatic Constitution on Divine Revelation* from Vatican II: "God speaks in sacred Scripture through men in human fashion" (*Dei Verbum* 3/12; see also the Pontifical Biblical Commission 1994).

Lamentations models this theological process. Its speakers furiously and bitingly challenge their inherited understandings of God in light of their experiences of catastrophe, destruction, and annihilation. They express and then reject the Deuteronomistic and prophetic views that their suffering is their own fault. Even the strongman does this. They challenge God to be the deity who sees and responds to their particular woes. They accuse God of hiding from them, from their cries and prayers, and of refusing to forgive. They do not arrive at new understandings of the Ruler of the universe. The strongman haltingly reasserts traditional hopes, but he does not arrive at theological clarity, and the status of his hope remains suspect. The speakers' expressions of their experiences of pain, trauma, and loss offer a vigorous, critical, and "deconstructive" theology.

The speakers' present experience of tragedy and pain makes what they knew about God crumble and disintegrate. The wonder of this biblical book is its daring, momentous iconoclasm and is one reason we need the speakers' words about God's character. They show us how to do theology honestly, to take life's ingredients and to hold fast to the concrete realities of communal life. Every generation of believers and each local gathering of believers must engage in this task, or else they will make of the Living One an idol, a portrait of themselves, or a mere artifact of history. To deny these truthful voices equal weight with other biblical testimony is potentially to cut off our being, to deny dignity to the human sufferers, and to abort chances for healing.

No biblical portrayal of God exhausts God's being, maps God's identity, expresses for all times and all places in the same way who God is. We cannot simply and perpetually repeat biblical language from any text and think we have met God. We must always be alert to God's revelation in other biblical texts and to God who lives and speaks in the "texts" of our own times and places, of our own grief, losses, and doubts. Responsible theology requires critique of biblical speech about God and imaginative construction of new ways of meeting and speaking of God that let the biblical tradition live anew. It means hearing voices that challenge our notions of God. It requires Spirit-driven openness to divine revelation all around us. It requires contemplation of God met in our collective life as a community of believers, as a nation, as members of the global community.

The theological cold water of Lamentations offers a thread of hope, a slight parting of the veil of abuse and violence. The strongman asserts ambiguously, "For he [God] does not afflict willingly nor grieve the children of humans" (3:33). Although this puzzling formulation does not construct a new theology, it does suggest another way to imagine God. Rather than reinforcing God's abusiveness, this verse hints at God's powerlessness. It opens the possibility that God is unable to prevent evil. It points to a vulnerability in God, not as omniscient and omnipotent but as helpless in the face of forces, laws, or principles of creation already at work in the cosmos. The God who does not afflict or grieve willingly may be a God who cannot alter the forces at work in the world.

To this possibility I will cling as to a life raft upon a turbulent sea. For the time being I look to the God who suffers with the grieved and afflicted, a God whose power and sovereignty are not compromised by human suffering because God cannot prevent it.

This admittedly slim suggestion by the strongman enables me to imagine the Creator and Living One as one who rejects abusive and destructive powers of the world. It opens space for a God who is not abusive but grieving with the aggrieved and suffering with the oppressed. It suggests the possibility that even the divine silence in Lamentations may not reflect God's insensitivity and cruel harshness. It may suggest instead that God has no ready explanation for the catastrophes facing the beloved people. Instead, God suffers as the whole community accuses God of evil, hateful deeds. Maybe God's silence veils God's innocence rather than reveals divine calculated destructiveness. I want it to be so. I may thereby be suspect as an interpreter of God in this book.

Stammering toward the Unsayable

Still, the book leaves us only with the beautiful, culturally conditioned poetry that emerged from frightful destruction, pain, and suffering. The book's theologies of divine abuse represent stammering attempts to interpret their devastated world. We need those attempts for their iconoclasm and for their yearning for that divine presence as they search for words for unspeakable pain and unsayable mystery. They lead us toward silence and call us toward alert attention to the One who cannot ultimately be named.

Finally, we need these words because, in bold, courageous speech, these speakers blame God unequivocally. They are not silent, not denying, not accepting the blame and guilt that the abused often express before the abuser. Alice Miller's (1991, 114-126) interpretation of Lamentations is incomplete because she sees the speaker only as a victim. But the book's speakers stand up, resist, shout in protest, and fearlessly risk further antagonizing the deity. They do not accept abuse passively. They are voices of a people with nothing left to lose, and they find speech, face horror upon horror, and resist unsatisfactory interpretations offered by their theological tradition. From the authority of experience, they adopt a critical view and appraise and reappraise their situation. The result is a vast rupture in their relationship with God, yet they hold to God, and in that holding they clear space for new ways to meet God.

10

Prayer for the Wounded World

The book of Lamentations seems like the opposite of true worship. It attacks more than praises, doubts more than hopes. Filled with anger and outrage at God, its voices verge toward blasphemy. Yet more than anything else, Lamentations is an act of worship. It is prayer from within and for the world's brokenness. It can teach us how to pray.

The structuring heart of the book's poems is the lament form, complaints addressed to God. No matter the poetry's rebellious contents, Lamentations is worship, truth-filled and faithful prayer. Its forms and potent speech can speak on our behalf and show us how to compose our own prayers of lament in fearful times. It can encompass the world's enormous atrocities and its small tragedies. It can show us how to stand before God without pretension. By allowing us to be broken, angry, and tear-drenched before God, it can melt our hearts and become a vehicle of prayer for the wounds of the world.

The Lament Form

In some fashion each of Lamentation's poems contains essential elements of the lament form. Laments call on God, complain to God, and plead for intervention (Brueggemann 1984, 54; Miller 1994, 55-133; Pleins 13-44). Laments are purposeful acts "specifically intended to serve as intercession" (Frymer-Kensky 38). The poems of Lamentations reach toward God, yearn for God's attention, and speak as if with upraised arms to get God to pay attention, "to elicit divine compassion" (Dobbs-Allsopp 1997, 56). God's silence does not alter the prayerful nature of the book.

It would be easy to decide that, regardless of its conventional prayer forms, Lamentations still does not qualify as prayer because it attacks God. Even as rhetorical attempts to persuade God to move and to speak, the poems appear to be a sort of "anti-prayer." Their insulting challenges to the deity seem to reverse the worshipful purpose of lament—to express praise and trust in the midst of tragedy (Brueggemann 1984, 88; Miller 1994, 126). Speakers' dissatisfactions with God nearly overthrow the prayerful and worshipful intentions of the lament form. Complicating matters further, the poems in Lamentations are not consistently faithful to the lament form, omitting divine address (chapter 4) and, except for chapter 3, omitting words of assurance and vows of praise. Lamentations pushes lament beyond the traditional range of anger and despair.

By comparison, even Jeremiah's laments, often called confessions (Jer 1:8-12:6; 15:10-21; 17:14-18; 18:18-23; 20:7-13; O'Connor 1988; Diamond 1987) appear mild in their accusations against God. Jeremiah calls God a "deceitful brook" (Jer 15:18), charges God with seducing and raping him (Jer 20:7, my translation), and blames God for nourishing the wicked (Jer 12:1-2), but unlike Lamentations, he does not accuse God of direct attack. Only Job matches the venom and fury of Lamentations. He accuses God of lying in wait, of shooting poison-tipped arrows at him. But in the book of Job, God shows up, speaks to Job, and responds to Job's attack, no matter how ambiguously (Job 38:17-41:34).

But human words do not depend upon divine response to be authentic prayer. Often in the Hebrew Bible "the dialogue of prayer is painfully 'one-sided'" (Balentine 149). If laments express trust and hope in the midst of bare, ruined lives, Lamentations' very bleakness expresses fidelity. Its bitter accusations reveal profound yearning for God, even as God appears deeply untrustworthy and remote. It voices truth without which relationships cannot prosper.

Prayer as Truthfulness

Eastern theologian Raimon Panikkar says with utter simplicity, "Worship is above all, truthfulness" (Panikkar 41). If Panikkar is right, then Lamentations is deeply worshipful. Truth does not exist if pain cannot speak, nor is worship truthful if pain must be excluded. According to Holocaust survivor Theodor Adorno, the "need to let suffering speak is the condition of all truth" (Linafelt 2000, 1-2).

Lamentations meets both conditions for worship and truth-telling. It does nothing to cover pain, to "expunge it," or to belittle it. It presents and lays out the "aggressive presence of hurt and brokenness" (Linafelt 2000, 1-4). As if the entire community has descended into a permanent "dark night" of mind and body, Lamentations speaks of a tortured world that largely eclipses divine presence. The speakers doubt even the possibility of getting prayers through the impenetrable cloud in which God has wrapped the divine self (3:44). Yet they lay their suffering before God. They pray anyway.

Expression of pain is essential to prayer. It is that simple and that difficult. By telling the truth of its world to God, Lamentations becomes a school for prayer. Speaking truth to God can seem unthinkable, because God already knows, or because God may not care, or because God appears to be the cause of the trouble in the first place. But as in any relationship, not speaking truth to God causes a dwindling of mutuality and an expansion of anger, resentment, and alienation. Pray anyway.

Because Lamentations' speakers proclaim unvarnished truth before God, the book is full to overflowing with worshipful fidelity. Truth-telling is faithful to the "Other" because speakers of truth hold the relationship open from their side. They keep communicating as if the Other might finally respond. Of course, the speakers persistently express distrust of God's intentions. They accuse God of doing outright evil against them. Only the speaker in chapter 3 uses explicit language of trust, but even he does so with intermittent, unsteady confidence. Lamentations' speakers pray anyway. They proceed with the shaky hope that God hears them, that God is still open to them, that God can be persuaded to see. The lament form, more bleakly employed here than anywhere else in the Old Testament, is still prayer, desperate prayer, prayer abandoned to truth.

Except for the strongman (chapter 3), the speakers reverse usual perceptions of divine-human relationship. They cling relentlessly to God, but God betrays them. Their loyalty may be no more than the distorted devotion of the abused toward the Abuser (Miller 1991) or the pleas of the desperate with nowhere to turn. But it may also be steadfast fidelity to a relationship once glorious but now turned sour and ending. Poet and Holocaust survivor Paul Celan asserts a similar fierce fidelity in his "Poem to Nelly Sachs."

> The talk was of your God, I spoke
> against him, I
> the heart that I had
> hope:
> for His highest, His deathrattled, His
> Angry word. (in Ezrahi 146)

In broken, disjointed speech Celan speaks against "your God" as if this were not his own God but some distant other deity. Yet he still hopes with the heart he once had, once because after the Holocaust he is no longer the same person. He hopes for a word, even angry, even "deathrattled," from that distant God. According to Hamburger, Celan negates and blasphemes to "be true to the experience of being God-forsaken." Yet he maintains "intimate dialogue with God characteristic of Jewish devotion" (Hamburger 17). Etched with desire for God, Celan's prayer pulsates with bitter fury. Wrenching and faithful, like Lamentations, it is prayer of the God-forsaken.

Lamentations as Impassioned Hope

Speakers in Lamentations tenaciously persist in trying to engage God. They make claims on God, demand attention, and beg for a future. They do this even as God walks away and silently closes the door on them. God may be unfaithful, but they are faithful. God may hide, but they stand in plain view. They berate God, protest God's work, and dare to ask for more than patent cruelty. Lamentations is a bare act of hope and a plea for life.

Even in the face of God's silence, the speakers persevere. Their hope resides in the strongman's words for whom, at least briefly, God's mercies are "new every morning" (3:22-23). Hope resides in the broken, desperate pleas of Daughter Zion, who begs God to see (1:9c, 11c, 20; 2:20); in the urgings of the narrator, who tells her to weep day and night (2:18-19); and in the voices of the community, who plead with God to "return us to yourself" (5:21).

If, as Elizabeth Barrett Browning's poem "Grief" proclaims, passion is a barometer of hope, then Lamentations' speakers exude hope.

> I tell you, hopeless grief is passionless;
> That only men incredulous of despair,
> Half-taught in anguish, through the midnight air
> Beat upward to God's throne in loud access
> Of shrieking and reproach.

The speakers' excess of passion beats upward to God's throne in "loud access of shrieking and reproach." They batter God with insistence and accusation. They refuse God's refusal. In the midst of their collective midnight they cry out, reveal themselves, open outward. If and when God is ready to renew relationship, so are they. By dint of persistence and loud shrieking, they express their grief with impassioned hope.

Lamentations prays hopefully because it neither dodges truth nor lets God escape unchallenged into the cloudy heavens. In the face of pain and suffering, the speakers pray anyway. They challenge God and demand justice. Their truthfulness is piercing fidelity to a silent and withholding Other.

Lamentations as a Work of Justice

Prayers of lament in general and Lamentations in particular make space for justice to be born. To lament is to complain, to object, and to resist. It is to demand from God a new reality. Bell hooks shows what happens to justice in African-American communities when there is no place to lament:

> The absence of public arenas where pain could be articulated, expressed, and shared meant that it was held in—festering, suppressing the possibility that this collective grief would be reconciled in the community even as ways to move beyond it and continue resistance struggle would be envisioned . . . a life-threatening despair took hold in black life. (hooks 1994, 245)

Without the practice of public lament, collective work for justice is blocked, paralyzed, unable to begin.

Unlike other biblical prayers of praise and thanksgiving, laments announce aloud and publicly what is wrong right now. Laments create room within the individual and the community not only for grief and loss but also for seeing and naming injustice. Laments name the warping and fracturing of relationships—personal, political, domestic, ecclesial, national, and global. The point of lamenting is not to confess sin, though such confession deserves an honored place in liturgy (Billman and Migliore 14), but to name injustice, hurt, and anger.

Prayers of lament are not about what is wrong *with us* but about wrong done *to us*. They tell in specific ways how sin, evil, and deprivation harm human life and the earth itself. They point to all that destroy our abilities "to survive, dream . . . and to flourish" (Chopp 1995, 58). When people live in conditions that deprive them of dignity, of control of their bodies, of what they need to eat and clothe themselves, or of what they need to flourish in mind and spirit, they need to lament. Laments make "spaces of recognition and catharsis" (Chopp 1993, 13) that prepare for justice.

To borrow a phrase from the Catholic Worker movement, laments aid in "clarification of thought." Whether traditional or newly composed, prayers of lament articulate in precise ways how things have fallen apart. Brought before God, they enable us to see clearly what is wrong, to specify fractures in systems and relationships that destroy us, and to realize ourselves how our lives are barren.

Laments empower sufferers to speak for themselves. When we tell how desperate we are, we become actors in the world. No longer passive recipients of pain, we become agents who name and interpret reality. Slowly such speaking may alter our relationship to suffering and release energies to act. Naming suffering before God reclaims human dignity and power that has been trampled and violated. Speaking pain, perhaps repeatedly, "like a broken record," can move sufferers toward healing, because it brings denial to a halt and enables truth to come to the surface.

Acts of lamenting help us see our lives with clarity and become our own witnesses. Because lamenting brings fuller recognition of the world as it actually is, it sets free unknown resources and passions for living and for justice. It can overcome the paralysis inflicted by trauma, oppression, and abuse. Laments are the beginning of action, a rejection of passivity, and so they can invert despair. Across the spectrum of pain, across intersections of personal and political domains, lamenting releases life for life.

Gregory Nagy asks if there is any way societies can abort endless cycles of retaliation, of ever-new wrongs committed to avenge the past. He observes that the "absolute grief and absolute anger" that follow upon murder and warfare can be never be erased from the mind. These emotions are "the wellspring of lament," and they "become the ultimate justification for revenge, for the spirit of the vendetta, for the horrors of retaliation against earlier horror. Is there any social solution?" (in Loraux xii).

It would be naive in the extreme to claim that Lamentations and other laments can stop hatred and retaliation. But without laments, without truth-telling received by compassionate listeners, without pain brought to the open, seen and heard, paid attention to and acknowledged, without the work of witnessing there will never be a social solution. New social arrangements cannot be born. Lamentations is a vital resource for the work of peace and reconciliation.

The Power of Tears

Lamentations in particular and laments in general can unleash tears. They mirror suffering and expose wounds. They bring painful memories to light and provoke the unbidden bodily response of weeping. Thomas Aquinas spoke of "the gift of tears," the catharsis, the comfort, and the renewal that can come from expressing deep grief. For him, tears were a spiritual gift, a grace. But in the dominant culture of the United States, we generally consider public and private stoicism to be a sign of strength and dignity, no matter the loss (Walton 23-24). We often belittle tears as signs of weakness and inadequacy, allowing them only to women and children. This may be because if men were encouraged to weep, if men and women in power positions were to weep, they would then have access to their full humanity and the world would change. Tears are powerful, not weak.

Weeping as a Political Act

Theologian C. S. Song relates a Chinese parable about the power of tears (38-41). A young couple was separated on their wedding day by the military, who forced Lady Meng's new husband to join the laborers building China's Great Wall. Like many others, the husband never returned. Strong men went in search of the lost laborers and failed to find them or their remains. But when Lady Meng stood before the wall, her tears alone were strong enough to cause the wall's collapse and to reveal the bones of the dead who built it.

Lady Meng's tears were deeply personal, but they were also an act of political resistance. Her public, wordless lament unsettled the world's order. Her tears revealed rulers' atrocities and exposed the bones of the enslaved. With her weeping, the cover-up was ended, destroyed by a woman's powerful tears.

Tears, of course, mean many things and can follow upon any intense feelings. But the tears of Lamentations are of loss and grief, abandonment and outrage. They are a flag, a sign, a revelation of injury and destruction, an expression of resistance to the world's arrangements. They are also a release, an emptying, a cleansing of body and spirit (Leavitt 84). Lamentations validates tears. It has the power to gather bitter pain and bring tears to the surface. Then it accepts them.

Tears can give watery birth to hope. They can wash out space once occupied by despair, fury, or sorrow, and in that space hope can emerge uninvited. Hope comes apart from human will, decision, or optimism. It comes as a gift out of despair, as it did for the strongman in the bottom of the pit (Lam 3).

Tears need reverent, tender treatment, because they express what bodies know without words. They well up spontaneously, and only violence can prevent or dispel them. And God honors tears, preserves them, and records them in a book, says the Psalmist:

> You have kept count of my tossings;
>   put my tears in your bottle.
> Are they not in your record? (Ps 56:8, NRSV)

God receives and tenderly holds tears as if they are precious, explosive testimony that must be preserved for some future day. Perhaps this vigilant, seeing, and tear-collecting God weeps with the weeping world. Lamentations does not say this, of course, but it honors tears, and the book itself is a "sacred bottle" for the tears of the world. It records them in a book, respects them, keeps account of them to present to God when God is ready to receive them.

Prayers of Lament Teach Resistance

To lament is to pray in a spirit of resistance. Because it denounces abusive power, Lamentations teaches resistance. More thoroughly than any other biblical book, it challenges God's governance of the world. It refuses to accept a view of the world where God fixes everything, for God has not done so. It boldly asserts that divine governance has been a life-destroying failure. Because God kills without pity (3:43), because God has abandoned justice and mercy, the community must protest, resist, and reject.

Walter Brueggemann observes that psalms of lament teach resistance to any inappropriate uses of power. When laments rebuke God for the way things are, they alter the "calculus of power" in the divine-human relationship. They challenge the "unmitigated supremacy of the all powerful deity." When God "must be praised all the time," Brueggemann continues, prayer becomes a lie, a cover-up, and a warrant for the status quo. If believers are unable to challenge God "at the throne," other challenges "soon disappear in public places, in schools, in hospitals, with the government, and eventually in the courts" (Brueggemann 1986, 64). Or, as Balentine puts it, "If one cannot question God, to whom does one direct the questions?" (5).

By urging truth-telling before the powerful, and providing language, form, and practice of defiance, Lamentations encourages resistance and promotes human agency. But what can this mean in a wealthy, secure country where as a people we suffer from an excess of power? My answer is simple. Without coming to grips with our own despair, losses, and anger, we cannot gain our full humanity, unleash our blocked passions, or live in genuine community with others. Lamentations untangles complex knots of grief, despair, and violent anger that pervade this society—a society that refuses woundedness, weakness, and hurt. We need to access our passions to become true moral agents. By calling us both inward and outward, Lamentations can melt frozen and numbed spirits.

"Healing is the first component in moving toward embracing justice and liberation," writes Diana Akiyama (162). Radical conversion to solidarity with the poor, afflicted, and brokenhearted are at the heart of the Christian life. Honored social teachings of the major religions, and of Roman Catholicism in particular, beckon us to lives of justice and love. Liberation theologians from the two-thirds world and within the United States call us to conversion. They implore us to see how our economic, cultural, and military domination contributes to the diminishment of lives around the globe.

Why then do so many churches and faith communities respond limply, in small pockets, and in scant ways? Orlando Costas speaks about the inability of Americans to understand the "content of their neighbors' cries" (104).

Costas means that we do not understand that we live within the network of global relations. We do not see how our power and wealth depend upon and contribute to powerlessness and poverty elsewhere.

Justice and Solidarity

There are deep, complex reasons for our inability to hear the content of our neighbors' cries, both nearby and faraway. My claim is that our depleted humanity thwarts our vision. Because we will not see our own personal and communal sufferings, we have no room for the suffering of others. We have no experiential basis for compassion, few resources for solidarity, no urging passions to live justly, and little incentive to see beyond our own upkeep.

When we deny pain, we become paralyzed by guilt or frozen in fear and indifference. The suffering of others cannot turn our spirits because our marble hearts defend against it lest our own worlds unravel before us. Justice and love must arise from genuine connection to others and not from "a projection of one's own grief or anger or overwrought sense of responsibility upon them" (Joyce 1993, 312). Guilt arising from a well-meaning, "prophetic" attempt to stir us to action provides insufficient motivation for sustained engagement with the world. In a similar vein intellectual argument from ecclesial documents or from pulpits cannot alone persuade us that our relationships with others are blighted and unjust (Cone 61-79). Our restless grief, our losses, and our brokenness are the deep wells from which we can learn and sustain compassion.

"We are reluctant to grieve our failures, especially our corporate and public limitations and losses" (Billman and Migliore 15). When we deny and silence aspects of our beings, we abort the very possibility of compassion. Lamentations may help us to reclaim our broken humanity and to bring to the surface our hidden despair and alienation for our sake and for the sake of the world.

Prayers for the World

Lamentations summons us beyond ourselves. It calls Christians to become the communion of saints, the church united, the body of Christ broken together, the sacrament of healing for the world. Prayers of lament invite us to gather up the wounds, anger, and violence of the world, together with our own sorrows, disasters, and doubts. With its harsh images of grief, desolation, and inhumanity in the destroyed city, Lamentations makes visible the pain of our neighbors near and far. It can bring before us the suffering of peoples whose worlds are literally represented in the world of the text. It can help us "to place our suffering in a larger context and experience a sense of connection with other suffering human beings amidst our own pain" (Billman and Migliore 123). Lamentations beckons us outward toward the world.

As the world impinges upon us with ever more insistence, it is difficult to hide from the atrocities and destruction daily inflicted across the globe. The numbing litany of horrors that spanned the twentieth century alone, from the Armenian genocide, to mass killings in Rwanda, Bosnia, Serbia, and Sierra Leone, to the deplorable plight of refugees swarming from places of conflict, to underlying melancholy of the immigrants and displaced persons, to the murders of children by children in U.S. schools—the woes of the world endlessly call for lamentation.

If Lamentations does not serve as prayer for us because our sorrows are truly trivial and mitigated by a cosseting joy and well-being, Lamentations still calls us urgently to prayer for and with those whose lives too readily coincide with the brutish conditions that punctuate the book.

Lamentations and Liturgical Prayer

Lamentations deserves a more prominent place in the liturgical life of believing Christian communities than it presently holds (Brueggemann 1986; Billman and Migliore 12-14). Unless public worship uses the book, most believers will have little or no contact with it. Its potent language and affecting forms, as well as its capacities to house sorrow and teach resistance, can assist us in coping with present despair or future grief. Without it we lack a profound resource for personal crises, family tragedies, and communal devastations. Without it our repertoire of prayer lacks a vehicle particularly suited to connect us to other peoples.

Liturgy that is honest and care-filled, whether simple or elaborate, high church or low church, can transform the world. Liturgy can also bore the living daylights out of the community, infuriate worshipers with its disregard for human realities, and leave participants more alienated than when they began (Hellwig v-x). But when liturgy is authentic and, yes, beautiful, it honors lives of the worshipers and connects them to God, to one another, and to the world.

Lamentations should have a central place in worship because it can be a mirroring witness for those who live with untold sorrow and doubt. It can be a treasure stored in our spirits for the days to come. It can lead us through our sorrow and connect us in compassion to our neighbors. It provides a web of words, images, and vignettes that can in turn spawn new laments. Like all speech in a community of meaning, Lamentations can set free new speech that builds upon and recasts the ancient text in new laments, new literary worlds that make life visible and bearable for the afflicted.

Lamentations has an honored place in Jewish liturgy for the ninth of *Ab (Tisha B'av)*, a fast day that occurs in late July or early August. The day commemorates several events: the destruction of the temple by the Babylonians in 587 B.C.E.; the destruction of the second temple by the Romans in 70 C.E.; the expulsion of the Jews from Spain in 1492; and the Holocaust in the twentieth century (Waskow 215). And Lamentations has survived and been reclaimed and reconfigured over and over in Jewish religious and secular writings (Linafelt 2000).

Naomi Seidman writes about how the public reading draws her into the text in complicated ways.

> [The verses of Lamentations] are mine, but also not mine. . . . If I feel my own distance from the twisted wreck of Jerusalem as a kind of comfort, there is also discomfort and danger in this distance. If I am also a broken-down, lonely survivor of a disgraced city, if I can feel the shame of her nakedness, feel myself caught with a telltale patch of blood on my skirt, the equally terrible possibility exists that I am also the revolted lover slamming the door, the jeering witness. Worse, I am the stupid child bawling for her supper as the city burns. (Seidman 285)

Seidman's experience of the text suggests how public readings can engage hearers. The text invites Seidman into a world that simultaneously challenges, comforts, and endangers her. Aspects of her being find echoes in an expanded vision of herself within the context of Jewish worship and history.

In contrast to Judaism and Christianity, Islam does not employ the book of Lamentations in its religious services, nor do laments appear in the Islamic scriptures, the Qur'an. Laments, however, abound in the general culture (J. Kaltner, personal communication). Recited at times of death or during other crises, they have influenced the development of Islamic thought and spirituality (Renard 194). In Shi'ite Islam a lamentation commemorates the martyrdom of an important Islamic figure, the caliph Husayn, in 688 C.E. (Pinault 97-114).

In Christianity, Lamentations is largely reserved for funerals and for services on Holy Thursday and Good Friday. In a valid and rich use of the ancient text, Holy Week readings mourn the death of Christ. But when the book appears only then, worshipers may restrict the book's meanings to Christ's death and not as easily claim it as prayer for their sufferings and the sufferings of the world.

A number of Protestant biblical scholars mourn the scant use of lament psalms in their worship. Brueggemann bemoans their absence in worship services that offer only praise and obliterate troubles from public worship (Brueggemann 1986). R. B. Salters concurs: "It is perhaps difficult for us to appreciate a lament and its function in Israel in that we do not, as a rule, vent our anger or agony in worship" (100). Westermann adds to the complaint. The absence of lamentation from prayer means that "laments are not simply allowed to be laments. Either they are recast as something else or they are devalued for what they are" (1994, 82).

By contrast, in both Catholic and Protestant African-American churches, the spirit of lamentation is alive and well. People express anger and agony, joys and tears in their worship, and preaching often protests and resists. The context of the people, their long tradition of weeping and wailing in church, and the current discrimination, prejudice, and suffering among some impel lament. Cone writes, "Through sermon, prayer and song, we transcend societal humiliation and degradation. . . . Our church is the only place we can go with tears in our eyes without everyone asking 'what are you crying about?'" (Cone 130).

Until I began this study, I did not think the situation was quite so bleak in Roman Catholic eucharistic liturgies. To my surprise, I discovered that psalm responses to Sunday readings rarely include laments. Of course, members of religious orders and the clergy, as well as many members of the laity, daily recite the Liturgy of the Hours and, within the course of the year, read all one hundred fifty psalms. Spiritual directors and retreat directors recommend psalms of lament for personal prayer as well. But in my experience, Lamentations and lament psalms rarely appear in homilies or other forms of church teaching and worship, and when they do, they are usually understood only as prayers for the individual in need of God's swift intervention.

Roman Catholic funeral liturgy uses excerpts from Lamentations, usually selected from the few hopeful verses uttered by the strongman (3:21-33). The appropriateness of these words for funerals is evident; they proclaim an unseen future reliant upon a God of inexhaustible mercies. They give mourners hope for themselves and their deceased. But powerful as this text may be, it is not enough. It does not bring Lamentations into the hands of the bereft for the future time when the community no longer bears them up. It does not offer prayer for grieving or create space for wailing and weeping in loss and outrage.

Daring Prayer

Lamentations is prayer that, above all, urges truthfulness before God. No matter how debased, frightening, or banal our lives may appear, the book summons us to insist on our truth in all its concrete particularity and to place it before God. Despite our preconceptions of God's presence or absence, it teaches fierce staunchness before God. It encourages fidelity toward the Creator of the universe, no matter how faithless that Creator may be.

Even when uttered in the most spiteful, angry, and bitter tone, Lamentations urges us to present to God all that prevents full human flourishing—the wounds, despair, hatred, anger, and injustices of the world. It is prayer that is born in the deepest secrets of abandonment and loss. It expresses hungry, passionate yearning for God's presence. It is, therefore, enabling prayer that leaves no barrier between us and God. It goads God to speak. It urges God to reveal, to emerge from the clouds, and to comfort us. It dares God to be our witness and to restore us to God's own self. It is prayer for the in-between times of our relationship, and it will carry us through terror and despair to comfort, life, and wholeness.

Epilogue

The Comforting God

Comfort and healing do not arise from explicit themes, images, or promises in Lamentations but from the poetry's capacity to bear witness to pain. I have argued in this book that Lamentations' expressions of pain are sacred, comforting, and demanding all at once. They are sacred, not simply because they reside in a biblical text, but because they convey truth as the harsh testimony of survivors. They are comforting, not because they offer visions of hope beyond pain, but because their bare brutality and vulnerability see, face, and name pain. And they are demanding, not only because they hold before our eyes sorrow and collapse that we may prefer to deny, but because they create an ethical imperative; they command us to live as compassionate witnesses to suffering, our own and that of others.

Because it asserts and aggressively expresses pain in multiple voices and from several perspectives, Lamentations itself is a witness that comforts the oppressed and the wounded. Its stark vignettes, bitter tears, and angry cries leave pain open for view, like a wound exposed to air and light. Its metaphoric language enables it to embrace other sorrows, other losses, other catastrophes. And, its embrace of sorrow runs deep and wide, wide enough and deep enough to hold the tears of the world.

A Spirituality of Wholeness

Lamentations' poetry has this power because it is a work of art. Its acrostic and alphabetic structures build a roomy, poetic space, a world apart from our worlds, into which we enter with our tears, doubts, and furies. It embraces the brokenhearted and the despairing. It recognizes sorrow, despair, and dishonored humanity, allows them to be, and holds them reverently. Seen and accepted, we are no longer alone in our pain. We are safe in a symbolic environment that overcomes interpretive aggression and colonization by the well intentioned. We can discover language to bring voiceless pain to speech. We can learn from voices of resistance to name our worlds, to defy all that dehumanizes, and to become agents of wholeness.

In the process we can rescue our full selves from the thin veil of despair that stretches over this culture, a despair hidden by the allure of things, by drives to accomplish and to acquire, by frenzied days, and by our bullying, violent power in the world. In such a culture denial of pain is necessary to keep the whole edifice in place, but the accompanying exhaustion of our spirits, cut off from our deep roots, is enormous.

> We cut ourselves off from our own experiences by looking upon them as irrelevant and not worth talking about or, what is no less cynical, not communicable at all. We are losing dreams, those of the night, and those of the day, and increasingly we lose the visions of our life. (Soelle 14)

Lamentations encourages us to take our individual lives seriously, for they are a primal source of energy, hope, and healing not for ourselves alone, but for the community and the world. Without our "selves" we live half lives and have no heart for compassionate engagement with the world. Without our "selves," we are cut off from deep experiences of God's freedom and love.

A Summons to Companionship

Lamentations is not about the individual, except in a symbolic or metaphoric sense, but rather about the destruction of a people and its habitat. It calls us to prayer for peoples across the globe whose spiritual and material realities are graphically evoked by the poetry. It summons us to companionship with those whose homes and cities are destroyed, whose bodies are tortured, and whose spirits are depleted, colonized, and dehumanized. It urges practices of compassionate witnessing wherein we are able to see, hear, and accept pain and to be converted by the faithfulness and forgiveness of the victims. It invites us to empathic understanding wherein we do not interpret others' worlds for them but, from the breadth of our own beings, accept their naming of their world.

The haunting voices of Lamentations demand more of us than spiritual attentiveness to the beauty and grace of the world. They insist upon wide-open alertness to the world's small sorrows and massive atrocities. They demand that we become witnesses, even by simple acts of reading and praying the text. They invite us to become empathic witnesses who resist with all our might whatever harms life, violates human dignity, and defaces the earth. The voices of Lamentations resist God's abusiveness, shout down God's violence, and say no to a theology that blames them for the world's wrongs. They encourage us to gain our voice, to speak truth, to take rightful personal and collective power and use it for the flourishing of all God's creatures.

Theological Betweenness

Lamentations is a theological watershed, an in-between place where the old theology of a punishing God no longer holds but new understandings have not yet emerged. The people have come to an impasse, yet they long unceasingly for God's presence. But it is only because God's voice is largely missing from these poems that they are able to honor these voices of yearning and resentment. Whatever God's silence signifies, it assures that we will not be able to skip over or deny the cries of suffering and hopelessness. These voices are holy ground upon which God does not intrude.

But if God's silence honors the voices of suffering, the suffering voices return little honor to God. Instead, they accuse God of abusive and murderous cruelty. The abuse by God in Lamentations troubles many people and contributes to the book's unpopularity. But this harsh speech clears away theological debris, undercuts the pieties of civil religion and of a national God devoted exclusively to our prosperity. It makes God a free being unchained from our well-being. But God's freedom in Lamentations comes at a cost because it is couched in terms of violence and destruction. Even if this violent destructiveness could be construed as belonging to God alone, it still portrays an arbitrary God without ethical restraint who acts from on high with no regard for consequences.

A Biblical Response

The Bible itself responds to the abusing God of Lamentations with the comforting God of Second Isaiah. Second Isaiah (Isa 40-55) is an anonymous prophet whose work was added to the book of Isaiah (Isa 1-39), an eighth-century B.C.E. prophet in Jerusalem. Although historical dating of biblical books currently finds little consensus among interpreters, Second Isaiah was probably written, at least in part, at the end of the exilic period in Babylon (around 538 B.C.E.).

The text of Lamentations "survives" in Second Isaiah (Linafelt 2000, 62-79); indeed, Second Isaiah quotes, alludes to, and responds to Lamentations in a reconfiguration of characters and story for a different set of circumstances. Its allusions, quotations, and connections to Lamentations are too extensive to be accidental (Somer; O'Connor 1999). Second Isaiah's sequel to Lamentations revivifies Daughter Zion on her hill of weeping and changes God's character from abuser to comforter. In Second Isaiah God is present, vocal, and repentant.

Despite its more palatable nature, language of the God who comforts is, like abusive speech about God, also culturally conditioned speech, arising from its own historical time and place. It does not automatically supplant language of divine violence within the Bible. Instead, it stands alongside it in unresolved contradiction in an ongoing biblical conversation about the character of God in relation to God's people. My preference for Second Isaiah's depiction of God arises from my context, personal and cultural. I think violence drenches and divides the United States and that despair and alienation oppress our souls. In such a world and on my own path toward wholeness, Second Isaiah's way of portraying God appeals, for God repents of violence and abandonment. God stands on the side of the suffering Zion and reaches toward the grieved and afflicted as compassionate witness, although not unambiguously.

Many biblical texts portray God as a comforting witness who sees the afflicted and hears their cries. When Hagar is lost in the wilderness, for example, God hears her cries, speaks to her, and promises to make a great nation of her through the child in her womb (Gen 16:7-13). When Hebrew slaves in Egypt cry out, God hears their groaning, looks upon them, and takes notice of them (Ex 2:23-25; 3:9-12). And even in Lamentations, the strongman proclaims that God sees his affliction and hears his cries (3:57-63). But Second Isaiah emphatically and explicitly portrays God as comforter of Zion and her exiled children. God sees, hears, and acts for them according to her terms as she expressed them in Lamentations. God is the witness she begged for but did not find in Lamentations.

With clear political intent Second Isaiah writes to the exiles in Babylon. He wants to stir up rebellion, hope, and resolve among them for a return to the destroyed city. This hope becomes a possibility, because Persia is about to replace defeated Babylon as the ruling empire, and Persia's ruler, Cyrus, will issue an edict in 538 B.C.E., allowing exiles to return home. But Jerusalem lies in ruins, people who were not exiled have taken over the land, and the exiles themselves have settled down in Babylon. Return seems impossible, far worse than remaining.

With some of the most potent rhetoric in the Bible, Second Isaiah makes visible hope, beauty, and the alluring possibility of return and restoration. For this prophet of the exile, only return will ensure the survival of the believing community. To overcome resistance, to awaken and instill enthusiasm, and to prepare them to return, he revivifies Daughter Zion as a restored and repopulated city. He makes the city woman whole again, so she can stand up and welcome her lost children home. He takes her theological claims in Lamentations seriously and responds to them by reimagining God's character as the one who supplies her needs, who has heard her experience, and who acts according to her requests. She, in turn, becomes a beacon of hope for the nation's restoration.

Zion's Long Struggle

Daughter Zion has a literary history that begins before we meet her in Lamentations. The prophets Hosea and Jeremiah adapt an ancient Near Eastern concept of the gods' marriages and use it to explain the collapse of Israel and Judah to foreign invaders. Jeremiah associates Daughter Zion with God's wife Judah (O'Connor 1999, 282-286). Hosea begins the biblical story of God's broken household when God marries an unfaithful wife, Israel, who betrays him and pursues another lover (Hos 2). God tries to win her back, but only after capturing her and coercing her. Hosea uses the metaphor of God's broken marriage to the nation to claim that the fall of Israel was God's punishment for infidelity. Hosea's metaphor defends God from charges of injustice, for God is the brokenhearted lover, betrayed in the most intimate of ways by the beloved. Clearly woman Israel deserves her fate (Diamond and O'Connor).

To interpret the fall of Judah and Jerusalem, Jeremiah adapts the metaphor and adds new episodes to the story (Jer 2:1-4:2). Wife Judah is even more unfaithful than her sister, flagrantly pursuing other lovers (Jer 3:6-10), so God divorces her (Jer 3:1-5). For Jeremiah, Judah and Daughter Zion are essentially one entity, described with geographic breadth as Judah or more narrowly as the capital city Jerusalem.

After the divorce God sends a mythic army, called the "foe from the north," to attack and destroy the city woman (cf. Jer 4:5-7; 4:14-17; 4:19-20, 29-31; 5:7-11; 6:2-8; 8:18-9:3; 10:19-24; 12:7-13; 13:20-27; O'Connor 1998c; 1999, 284-285). The "foe from the north," ultimately identified as Babylon (Jer 20:1-6), acts as God's instrument to punish unfaithful Zion. The results are a broken marriage, a disrupted family, and a destroyed household. (Because God's role is that of husband in these texts, I will use masculine pronouns from time to time in the following sections.)

The Period of Divorce

Although Lamentations uses little marital language, it assumes the divorce has occurred and tells of its wreckage. Zion's foe has broken down the city walls and taken away her children. Her lovers have abandoned her, God has cast her off, and she suffers unspeakably with no one to comfort her. To punish her for her infidelities, God rejects her, casts off her children, and sends enemies against her (O'Connor 1999, 285). Zion never denies her complicity in the disaster, but she and the narrator insist that God is the betrayer who destroys pitilessly and disregards the one to whom he does this.

Viewed against Zion's literary history, Second Isaiah's poems of Zion come alive as a sequel to her story in Lamentations. They depict God recovering from past violence and angry excess to make a future of familial and material well-being for her. They contribute to a theology of witness because in them God enacts the role of witness. God sees, hears, and responds to her with receptive, empathetic attention. God recognizes the depth and breadth of her suffering and speaks to her of its enormity. It is as if her suffering in Lamentations converted God, turned God's spirit away from violence and toward compassion. The previously silent God speaks to her and acts on her behalf. In Second Isaiah, God gives her everything she demanded but did not receive in Lamentations. God is her comforter.

Although the poems of the Suffering Servant (Isa 42:1-9; 49:1-12; 50:4-11; 52:13-53:12) dominate Christian interpretations of Second Isaiah, Zion shares equal poetic status with him (Gottwald 1992; 1985, 497-502). She is a direct recipient of the book's announcements in the opening poem (40:1-2), appears in several poems (40:9; 41:27; and 51:1-16), and is the central personified figure in three poems (Isa 49:13-50:3; 51:17-52:12; and 54:1-17) that alternate with the Servant poems (O'Connor 1998c; Newsom 1992; Tull-Willey; Linafelt 2000, 65-79).

God's first act of witnessing is to speak words of comfort to her and to admit the excesses of her punishment.

> Comfort, O comfort my people,
>   says your God.
> Speak tenderly to Jerusalem
>   and cry to her
> that she has served her term,
>   that her penalty is paid,
> that she has received from the LORD's hand
>   double for her sins. (Isa 40:1-2, NRSV)

God's double command to comfort Zion, front and center in Second Isaiah's opening words, expresses an urgency on God's part (Westermann 1969, 34) and affirms Zion's own assessment of her suffering in Lamentations. God concedes: it is excessive, it is double, and it is from God. In the three large poems devoted to Zion at the book's end, God comforts her and piece by piece reassembles her life and restores their broken household.

Reunion of Mother and Children (Isa 49:13-50:3)

God peremptorily opens the first long poem of Zion with a startling command to the heavens, the earth, and the mountains to sing, celebrate, break out in joy, for God has comforted the people (49:13). But Zion interrupts this cosmic rejoicing with a sharp rebuke that reprises the community's prayer at the end of Lamentations (5:20). God "has forsaken me" and "has forgotten me," she objects (Isa 49:14), as if demanding an apology and doubting God's capacity to comfort anyone. God responds, speaking directly to her and in a manner that bears witness to her world of loss:

> Can a woman forget her nursing child
>   or show no compassion for the child of her womb?
> Even these may forget,
>   yet I will not forget you. (Isa 49:15, NRSV)

This city woman, whose children have been violently torn from her, must answer God's questions with a resounding "No!" A mother never forgets her child, but how could this abusive God consider himself to be anything like a compassionate mother?

Then God adds promises of action to his words of remembrance. He tells the city woman that he has inscribed her walls "on the palms of my hands" (Isa 49:16, NRSV). The blueprint of her reconstruction already exists, tattooed on God's body. Look, the builders are already approaching. And in a complete reversal of her presumed fate, God's words reach to her deepest wound. With heart-stopping effect, he promises to bring back her lost children. They will be so numerous, they will complain about lack of space (49:17-20). The woman who said, "I was bereaved. . . . I was left all alone," will wonder in astonishment, "where then have these come from?" (49:21, NRSV). God is signaling the nations to return her children to her (49:22-26).

Then God speaks to the children (50:1-3), and his words revise and reconfigure Zion's story. Where is their mother's bill of divorce? Has God torn it up? Did the divorce never happen? The children have misinterpreted their mother's story and their own as well. It was not their mother's sins that brought exile upon them but their sins that brought disaster upon her. In direct alteration of Zion's story, God revises history. She is not to blame; they are. God is still blaming, but Zion's own innocence is confirmed and the exiled generation can no longer blame its parent for its plight.

Zion's Husband Returns to Her (Isa 51:17-52:12)

In the next poem the witnessing God sees Zion's suffering and mirrors it back to her. The entire poetic section concerns Zion, but she does not appear in person until verse 17. God tells her that he knows how much she has suffered. He recognizes that she has drunk from Jeremiah's cup of staggering and destruction (Jer 25), and she has drunk it to the dregs, to the very bottom of pain (Isa 49:17). He notices that even though she bore many children, she is alone and, therefore, in danger.

God then echoes Lamentations, as if he had been listening and watching all along:

> Your children have fainted,
>> they lie at the head of every street. (Isa 51:20,
>> NRSV; cf. Lam 2:11; 4:1)

His words acknowledge her pain, and he admits her children suffered because he was angry. Now he will plead for her, take the cup from her, and give it to her tormentors. He affirms that her enemies dehumanized her and that she endured through it:

> You have made your back like the ground
>> and like the street for them to walk on. (Isa 51:23,
>> NRSV)

He sees her as she is.

God's comforting of Zion in this poem is more subtle than the comforting return of her children in the previous poems but no less important. Testifying to the vastness of her pain, God validates her, affirms her interpretation of her reality. This means her isolation is over, at least for the moment. Then he returns to her side:

> . . . Together they sing for joy;
> for in plain sight they see
>> the return of the LORD to Zion.
> . . . for the LORD has comforted his people,
>> he has redeemed Jerusalem. (Isa 52:8-9, NRSV)

Family Reconciliation (Isa 54:1-17)

In the final Zion poem God commands Zion to sing, for her world is about to change. He addresses her as "barren one," again recognizing her world of loneliness and loss. Soon she will have to enlarge her tents to make room for her children for they will be so many (Isa 54:1-3). The disgrace of her widowhood is over, and she will forget her shame, for her husband has returned to her. He recognizes that she is forsaken and grieved in spirit, "like the wife of a man's youth when she is cast off" (Isa 54:6, NRSV). Then he admits what she knew all along—he abandoned her:

> For a brief moment I abandoned you,
>   but with great compassion I will gather you.
> In overflowing wrath for a moment
>   I hid my face from you,
> but with everlasting love I will have compassion on
>   you. (Isa 54:7-8, NRSV)

Zion's depiction of her suffering in Lamentations was completely accurate. He abandoned her; he hid from her, not the other way around. God has confessed anger and abandonment and now promises eternal love.

God Rebuilds the City

God, her seeing witness, acknowledges her suffering by calling her "afflicted one, storm-tossed, and not comforted" (54:11, NRSV). Now God promises to rebuild the city in antinomy, sapphires, rubies, jewels and precious stones, more beautiful than she could ever imagine (54:11-12). Her children will live in prosperity, and fear and oppression will be far from her.

God sees her reality, is changed by it, and acts to reverse it. In the context of the ancient world, God has comforted her, made room for healing, and set in motion a new future. She, in turn, has survived. Her mourning is turning to dancing and her sorrow to joy. Or so we imagine, for the text gives little of her response. The ancient world would assume her joy. The family and its dwelling place are restored, and the marriage begins again.

God Is Her Witness

In these poems God is Zion's comforting witness. God takes her distress into the divine consciousness, affirms its totality, and names its features as she named them in Lamentations. God sees her suffering, the loss of her children, her shame and humiliation, the violence of her enemies, her grieving and storm-tossed soul. God speaks to her, acts to reverse her afflictions, and confesses to abandoning her. According to marriage arrangements and gender understandings in the ancient world, all is well in this restored household. God reinstates city woman Zion as a woman of honor. Her divine husband realizes he erred in disciplining her, and the family is whole again.

But from the perspective of contemporary gender relations and abuse theory, all may not be well in this poetic family. Even as Second Isaiah's poems of Zion reverse her tribulations in Lamentations, they may also reinforce patterns of domestic abuse. Often in domestic relationships abusers repent after battering and with affecting words and gestures promise never to batter again, only to repeat the pattern in a still more vicious cycle of abuse. Is this pattern of violence inscribed in the Zion poems, or is the relationship of God to Daughter Zion set on a new footing in Second Isaiah? The text assumes she wants her husband back and that she is pleased with his arrangements for her and her children. Does the divine husband's repentance indicate a renunciation of further violence against her?

Sandra Winter, a participant in one of my classes on Lamentations, suggests comparing Zion's situation to the situation of Korean "comfort women." These women prefer the more descriptive term "sex slaves," for they were forced to give their bodies to Japanese military during World War II. Winter's study identifies what the Korean women ask for as adequate reparation from Japan. They want a public apology, some solemn words that recognize and witness to their suffering. But words are not enough. They also want some public gesture, some explicit, physical sign—perhaps a monument—that official Japan knows it dehumanized them and will refrain from such practices ever after.

Winter wonders if the rebuilding of Jerusalem in the Zion poems might signify for us such a public gesture on the part of God. Could the city's restoration in jewels and fine stones stand for a repentant heart, deep sorrow, and a firm purpose of amendment in which abuse comes to an end? I wonder, too.

Second Isaiah's Zion poems respond directly to Lamentations. That God is the dominant speaker is less troublesome to me than to Tull-Willey, who notes Zion's silence in Second Isaiah (303). After Zion protests God's claim to be a comforter by accusing God of forgetting and abandoning her (Isa 49:13-14), she speaks only one more time, to exclaim in joy about her children (49:21). She is not completely silent, but now it is God's turn to speak, to explain, to apologize, and to address her with words of comfort.

Second Isaiah is able to shift the focus from Zion's affliction and despair to God's comfort only because Lamentations created a house for sorrow. Because Lamentations gives suffering expression, because abandonment and loss, grief and rage come to voice, and because tears and rage and despair receive a place of honor in Lamentations, Second Isaiah can sing of comfort, of rebuilding, of a new world ahead. Only after the intense, pain-filled, and despairing poetry of Lamentations can the community begin to set the catastrophe into a larger theological framework.

Zion and the Suffering Servant

In many ways Zion is a parallel figure to the Suffering Servant (Isa 42:1-9; 49:1-12; 50:4-11; 52:13-53:12) with whom her poems are juxtaposed and interact. Both are figures of appalling suffering, survivors who endure to see a new future. But Zion's differences from the Servant are the most revealing. Unlike the Servant's suffering, her sufferings are over, her future already dreamed of, and her reasons for joy are concrete and palpable. She is a figure of healing; her new life is already anticipated. As capital city, monarchical center, and divine dwelling place, her restoration and renewal lure the exiled children homeward. She is already standing to receive them. Risen from the dust, she waits for them in longing anticipation. Perhaps she can become their comforting witness. Having plumbed her suffering so deeply, brought it to voice, shouted it at her betraying God, she can now see, pay attention, and be a comforter for her returning inhabitants. Perhaps in the world of imaginative poetry, she can help them regain dignity and community.

Even though in Second Isaiah Zion fades as active speaker and as God's accusing, demanding critic, she remains a central figure in the text, the one to be appeased and pleased. God acknowledges, addresses, and reverses her sufferings. Her guilt virtually disappears, and God, not she, is on the defensive. She has named her world in Lamentations, and now God responds on her terms, using her language, and giving her what she needs and more.

Second Isaiah presents the other side of the conversation. The book transforms her from a devastated, shamed, and abandoned woman into the central member of a family, with her children bursting out around her. She is the future. Her revivification lures the exiles homeward. Second Isaiah has already imagined her new life, laid it before the exiles as it is about to be realized. Her lamentations are over, her mourning has become dancing, and joy washes away despair.

Bibliography

Achtemeier, P.J. 2000. *The Harper Collins Bible Dictionary*. Rev. ed. San Francisco: Harper San Francisco.

Ackermann, D. 1996. "On Hearing and Lamenting: Faith and Truth-telling." In *To Remember and to Heal*, edited by H.R. Botman and R.M. Petersen, 47-56. Capetown: Human & Rousseau.

Akiyama, D.D. 1994. "Doing Theology toward Healing and Freedom: A Japanese American Woman's Perspective." In *Sisters Struggling in the Spirit: A Woman of Color Anthology*. Louisville, Ky.: Presbyterian Church (USA).

Albrektson, B. 1963. *Studies in the Text and the Theology of the Book of Lamentations with a Critical Edition of the Peshitta Text*. Studia Theologica Lundensia 21. Lund: CWK Gleerup.

Balentine, S.E. 1993. *Prayer in the Hebrew Bible: The Drama of Divine Human Dialogue*. Overtures to Biblical Theology. Minneapolis, Minn.: Fortress.

Ball, E. 1999. *In Search of True Wisdom: Essays in Old Testament Interpretation in Honour of Ronald E. Clements*. Journal for the Study of the Old Testament Supplement 300. Sheffield: Sheffield Academic Press.

Baumgartner, W. 1988. *Jeremiah's Poems of Lament*. English translation. Sheffield: Almond Press.

Bennett, M.J. 1998. "Overcoming the Golden Rule: Sympathy and Empathy." In *Basic Concepts of Intercultural Communication: Selected Readings*, edited by M.J. Bennett. Yarmouth, Maine: Intercultural Press.

Billman, K.D., and Migliore, D.L. 1999. *Rachel's Cry: Prayer of Lament and Rebirth of Hope*. Cleveland, Ohio: United Church Press.

Blenkinsopp, J. 1998. "The Judean Priesthood during the Neo-Babylonian and Achaemenid Periods: A Hypothetical Reconstruction." *Catholic Biblical Quarterly*: 25-43.

Blumenthal, D. 1993. *Facing the Abusing God: A Theology of Protest*. Louisville, Ky.: Westminster/John Knox.

Botman, H.R., and Petersen, R.M., eds. 1996. *To Remember and to Heal*. Capetown: Human & Rousseau.

Brenner, A., and van Dijk-Hemmes, F. 1996. *On Gendering Texts: Female and Male Voices in the Hebrew Bible*. Biblical Interpretation Series. Leiden: E.J. Brill, 83-90.

Brown, F., S.R. Driver, and C.A. Briggs. 1978. *Hebrew and English Lexicon of the Old Testament*. Oxford: Clarendon.

Brueggemann, W. 1984. *The Message of the Psalms: A Theological Commentary*. Minneapolis, Minn.: Augsburg.

———. 1986. "The Costly Loss of Lament." *Journal for the Study of the Old Testament*, 57-71. Reprinted in *The Psalms and the Life of Faith*, edited by P.D. Miller, 98-111. Minneapolis, Minn.: Fortress, 1995.

———. 1993. *Texts under Negotiation: The Bible and the Postmodern Imagination.* Minneapolis, Minn.: Fortress.

———. 1995. "The Formfulness of Grief." In *The Psalms and the Life of Faith,* edited by P.D. Miller, 84-97. Minneapolis, Minn.: Fortress.

———. 1997. *Theology of the Old Testament: Testimony, Dispute, Advocacy.* Minneapolis, Minn.: Fortress.

———, ed. 2001. *Hope for the World: Mission in a Global Context.* Louisville, Ky.: Westminster/John Knox.

Brunet, G. 1968. *Les Lamentations Contre Jeremie: Reinterpretation des Quartres Premieres Lamentations.* Science Religieuses 75. Paris: Presses Universitaires de France.

Bryan, A. 1999. "Theology and Art." Paper presented at the Weekly Forum, Columbia Theological Seminary, April 14.

Buchmann, D., and C. Spiegel, eds. 1992. *Out of the Garden: Women Writers on the Bible.* New York: Fawcett Columbine.

Camp, C. 1998. "1 and 2 Kings." In *The Women's Bible Commentary: Expanded Edition with Apocrypha,* edited by C. Newsom and S. Ringe. Louisville, Ky.: Westminster/John Knox.

Camus, A. 1957. *The Rebel: An Essay on Man in Revolt.* New York: Knopf, 263n. Quoted in S.D. Ezrahi. 1980. *By Words Alone: The Holocaust in Literature.* Chicago: University of Chicago Press.

Capps, D. 1992. *The Depleted Self: Sin in a Narcissistic Age.* Minneapolis, Minn.: Fortress.

Chastain, K.P. 1997. "The Dying Art of Demon-Recognition: Victims, Systems and the Book of Job." In *Power, Powerlessness, and the Divine: New Inquiries in the Bible and Theology,* edited by C. Rigby, 161-178. Atlanta, Ga.: Scholars Press.

Chopp, R. 1993. "Feminism and the Theology of Sin." *The Ecumenist* (November-December): 12-16.

———. 1995. *Saving Work: Feminist Practices of Theological Education.* Louisville, Ky.: Westminster/John Knox.

———. 2000. "The Theology and the Politics of Testimony." Paper presented at Emory University Law School.

Cone, J. 1986. *Speaking the Truth: Ecumenism, Liberation and Black Theology.* Maryknoll, N.Y.: Orbis Books.

Cooper, J. 1999. *The Flashboat: Poems Collected and Reclaimed.* New York: W.W. Norton.

Copeland, S. 1993. "'Wading through Many Sorrows:' Toward a Theology of Suffering in Womanist Perspective." In *A Troubling in My Soul,* edited by E.M. Townes. Maryknoll, N.Y.: Orbis Books.

Corley, K.E. 1998. "Women and the Crucifixion and Burial of Jesus." *Forum* (New Series) 1 (Spring): 181-225.

Costas, O.E. 1993. *Christ outside the Gate: Mission beyond Christendom.* Maryknoll, N.Y.: Orbis Books.

Cross, F.M. 1983. "Studies in the Structure of Hebrew Verse: The Prosody of Lamentations 1:1-22." In *The Word of the Lord Shall Go Forth: Essays in Honor of David Noel Freedman in Celebration of His Sixtieth Birthday,* edited by C.L. Meyers and M. O'Connor, 129-155. Winona Lake, Ind.: Eisenbrauns.

Darr, K.P. 1994. *Isaiah's Vision and the Family of God.* Louisville, Ky.: Westminster/John Knox.

Day, P.L., ed. 1989. *Gender and Difference in Ancient Israel.* Minneapolis, Minn.: Fortress.

Diamond, A.R.P. 1987. *The Confessions of Jeremiah in Context: Scenes of Prophetic Drama.* Journal for the Study of the Old Testament Supplement Series 45. Sheffield: JSOT.

Diamond, A.R.P., and K.M. O'Connor. 1999. "Unfaithful Passions: Coding Women Coding Men in Jeremiah 2:1-3:25 (4:2)." In *Troubling Jeremiah*, edited by A.R.P. Diamond et al., 387-403. Journal for the Study of the Old Testament Supplement 260. Sheffield: Sheffield Academic Press.

Diamond, A.R.P., K.M. O'Connor, and L. Stulman, eds. 1999. *Troubling Jeremiah.* Journal for the Study of the Old Testament Supplement 260. Sheffield: Sheffield Academic Press.

Dobbs-Allsopp, F.W. 1993. *Weep, O Daughter of Zion: A Study of the City-Lament Genre in the Hebrew Bible.* Biblica et Orientalia 44. Rome: Editrice Pontificio Istituto Biblico.

———. 1995. "*Bat* Followed by a Geographical Name in the Hebrew Bible: A Reconsideration of Its Meaning and Grammar." *Catholic Biblical Quarterly.* 451-470.

———. 1997. "Tragedy, Tradition, and Theology in the Book of Lamentations." *Journal for the Study of the Old Testament* 74: 29-60.

———. 1998. "Linguistic Evidence for the Date of Lamentations." *Journal of the Ancient Near Eastern Society* 26: 1-36.

———. Forthcoming. *Lamentations.* Interpretation Bible Series. Louisville, Ky.: Westminster/John Knox.

Eshel, H., and J. Strugnell. 1999. "Alphabetic Acrostics in Pre-Tannaitic Hebrew." *Catholic Biblical Quarterly.* 441-458.

Espín, O.O. 1999. "An Exploration into the Theology of Sin and Grace." In *From the Heart of Our People: Latino/a Explorations in Catholic Systematic Theology*, edited by O.O. Espín and Miguel H. Diaz. Maryknoll, N.Y.: Orbis Books.

Ezrahi, S.D. 1980. *By Words Alone: The Holocaust in Literature.* Chicago: University of Chicago Press.

Farley, W. 1990. *Tragic Vision and Divine Compassion: A Contemporary Theodicy.* Louisville, Ky.: Westminster/John Knox.

Ferris, P.W., Jr. 1992. *The Genre of Communal Lament in the Bible and the Ancient Near East.* Society of Biblical Literature Dissertation Series 127. Atlanta, Ga.: Scholars Press.

Fitzgerald, A. 1972. "The Mythological Background for the Presentation of Jerusalem as a Queen and False Worship as Adultery in the OT." *Catholic Biblical Quarterly.* 403-416.

Forché, Carolyn. 1993. *Against Forgetting: Twentieth Century Poetry of Witness.* New York: W.W. Norton.

Frank, A. 1996. *The Wounded Story Teller: Body Illness and Ethics.* Chicago: University of Chicago Press.

Freedman, S.G. 1997. "Laying Claim to Sorrow Beyond Words." *New York Times*, Arts and Ideas, National Edition (December 13): A11.

Fretheim, T.E. 1984. *The Suffering of God: An Old Testament Perspective.* Overtures to Biblical Theology. Philadelphia: Fortress.

Frye, N. 1957. *Anatomy of Criticism.* Princeton, N.J.: Princeton University Press.

Frymer-Kensky, T. 1992. *In the Wake of the Goddesses: Women, Culture, and the Biblical Transformation of Pagan Myths.* New York: Fawcett Columbine.

Gallagher, J., ed. 1966. *The Documents of Vatican II*. New York: Guild Press.

Gaughan, R.T. 1992. "'Man Thinks; God Laughs': Kundera's 'Nobody Will Laugh.'" *Studies in Short Fiction* 29, no. 1 (winter): 1-10.

Gordis, R. 1974a. "Critical Notes: The Conclusion of the Book of Lamentations (5:22)." *Journal of Biblical Literature*. 289-293.

———. 1974b. *The Song of Songs and Lamentations*. New York: KTAV.

Gottlieb, H. 1978. *A Study of the Text of Lamentations*. *Acta Jutlandica 48*. Theology Series 12. Arhus.

Gottwald, N.K. 1954. *Studies in the Book of Lamentations*. Chicago: Alec R. Allenson.

———. 1985. *The Hebrew Bible: A Socio-Literary Introduction*. Philadelphia: Fortress.

———. 1992. "Social Class and Ideology in Isaiah 40-55: An Eagletonian Reading." *Semeia* 59: 3-71.

———. 2000. "Lamentations." In *The Harper Collins Bible Commentary*, edited by James L. Mayes. San Francisco: HarperSanFrancisco.

Grossberg, D. 1989. *Centripetal and Centrifugal Structures in Biblical Poetry*. Society of Biblical Literature Monograph Series 39. Atlanta, Ga.: Scholars Press.

Guder, D. 1998. *Missional Church: A Vision for the Sending of the Church in North America*. Grand Rapids, Mich.: Eerdmans.

Gwaltney, W.C., Jr. 1983. "The Biblical Book of Lamentations in the Context of Ancient Near Eastern Lament Literature." In *Scripture in Context II: More Essays on the Comparative Method*, edited by W.W. Hallo et al. Winona Lake, Ind.: Eisenbrauns.

Hall, D.J. 2001. "Whether, or in What Sense, Despair May Be Regarded as the Spiritual Condition of Humankind at the Outset of the Twenty-First Century." A version is now found in *Hope for the World: Mission in a Global Context*, edited by W. Brueggemann. Louisville, Ky.: Westminster/John Knox.

Hallo, W., ed. 1983. *Scripture in Context II: More Essays on the Comparative Method*. Winona Lake, Wis.: Eisenbrauns.

Hamburger, P., ed. 1972. *Paul Celan: Selected Poems*. New York: Penguin.

Heim, K.M. 1999. "The Personification of Jerusalem and the Drama of Her Bereavement in Lamentations." In *Zion: City of Our God*, edited by R.S. Hess and G.J. Wenham. Grand Rapids, Mich.: Eerdmans.

Hellwig, M.K. 1992. *The Eucharist and the Hunger of the World*. 2d ed. New York: Sheed & Ward.

Hens-Piazza, G. 1998. "Forms of Violence and the Violence of Forms: Two Cannibal Mothers before a King (2 Kings 6:24-33)." *Journal for Feminist Studies in Religion* (Fall).

Herman, Judith Lewis. 1992. *Trauma and Recovery*. New York: Basic Books.

Heschel, A.J. 1962. *The Prophets*. 2 volumes. New York: Harper & Row.

Hess, R.S., and G.J. Wenham, eds. 1999. *Zion: City of Our God*. Grand Rapids, Mich.: Eerdmans.

Hiebert, P.S. 1989. "The Biblical Widow." In *Gender and Difference in Ancient Israel*, edited by P.L. Day, 125-141. Minneapolis, Minn.: Fortress.

Hillers, D. 1972. *Lamentations*. Anchor Bible 7a. Garden City: Doubleday.

hooks, b. 1994. "Love as the Practice of Freedom." In *Outlaw Culture: Resisting Representations*, 243-250. New York: Routledge.

———. 1999. "Love." Paper presented at Annual Meeting of the American Academy of Religion and the Society of Biblical Literature, Boston.

————. 2000. *All about Love: New Visions*. New York: William Morrow.

Joyce, P.M. 1993. "Lamentations and the Grief Process: A Psychological Reading." *Biblical Interpretation*. 304-320.

————. 1999. "Sitting Loose to History: Reading the Book of Lamentations without Primary Reference to Its Original Historical Setting." In *In Search of True Wisdom: Essays in Old Testament Interpretation in Honour of Ronald E. Clements*, edited by E. Ball. Journal for the Study of the Old Testament Supplement 300. Sheffield: Sheffield Academic Press.

Kaiser, B.B. 1987. "Poet as 'Female Impersonator': The Image of Daughter Zion as Speaker in Biblical Poems of Suffering." *The Journal of Religion* 67, no. 2: 164-182.

Kaiser, O. 1981. "Klagelieder." In *Spruche, Prediger, Das Hohe Lied, Klagelieder, Das Buch Esther*, edited by J. Ringren et al. ATD 16. Göttingen.

Kaltner, J. 1999. *Ishmael Instructs Isaac: An Introduction to the Qur'an for Bible Readers*. Collegeville, Minn.: Liturgical Press.

Lanahan, F.W. 1974. "The Speaking Voice in the Book of Lamentations." *Journal of Biblical Literature* 93: 41-49.

Lang, B., ed. 1988. *Writing and the Holocaust*. New York: Holmes and Meier.

Langer, L.L. 1991. *Holocaust Testimonies: The Ruins of Memory*. New Haven: Yale University Press.

————. 1995. *New Art from Ashes: A Holocaust Anthology*. Oxford: Oxford University Press.

Lasch, C. 1978. *The Culture of Narcissism: American Life in an Age of Diminishing Expectations*. New York: Norton.

Leavitt, J. 1998. "A Work of Lamentation." *Parabola: Myth, Tradition, and the Hand for Receiving* (Spring).

Lee, N. Forthcoming. *The Singers of Lamentations: Cities under Siege, from Ur to Jerusalem to Sarajevo*. London: E.J. Brill.

Leicht, V.B. 1992. *Cultural Criticism, Literary Theory, Poststructuralism*. New York: Columbia University Press.

Levine, Baruch A. 1993. "Silence, Sound, and the Phenomenology of Mourning in Biblical Israel." *Journal of Ancient Near Eastern Studies*: 89-106.

Lifton, R.J. 1982. "The Psychology of the Survivor and the Death Imprint." *Psychiatric Annals* 12, no. 11: 1011-1020.

Linafelt, T. 2000. *Surviving Lamentations: Catastrophe, Lament, and Protest in the Afterlife of a Biblical Book*. Chicago: University of Chicago Press.

————. 2001. "The Refusal of a Conclusion in the Book of Lamentations. *Journal of Biblical Literature* 120, no. 2: 340-343.

Linafelt, T., and T.K. Beal. 1998. *God in the Fray: A Tribute to Walter Brueggemann*. Minneapolis, Minn.: Fortress.

Linafelt, T., and F.W. Dobbs-Allsopp. 2001. "The Rape of Zion in Lam 1:10." *Zeitschrift für die alttestamentliche Wissenschaft*. Berlin: Walter de Gruyter.

Loraux, N. 1996. *Mothers in Mourning: Myth and Poetics*. Ithaca, N.Y.: Cornell University Press.

Macy, J. 1992. *World as Lover, World as Self*. Berkeley, Calif.: Parallax.McFarlane, G. 2000. "The Litmus Test of Trinitarian Talk: A Review Essay." *Catalyst* (April).

McKnight, Edgar. 1988. *Postmodern Use of the Bible: The Emergence of Reader-Oriented Criticism*. Nashville, Tenn.: Abingdon.

Meyer, L. 1993. "A Lack of Laments in the Church's Use of the Psalter." *Lutheran Quarterly* (Spring): 67-87.

Meyers, C.L., and M. O'Connor, eds. 1983. *The Word of the Lord Shall Go Forth: Essays in Honor of David Noel Freedman in Celebration of His Sixtieth Birthday.* Winona Lake, Wis.: Eisenbrauns.

Miller, A. 1979. *The Drama of the Gifted Child.* New York: Basic Books.

———. 1982. *For Your Own Good: Hidden Cruelty in Children and the Roots of Violence.* New York: Farrar, Straus and Giroux.

———. 1984. *Thou Shalt Not Be Aware: Society's Betrayal of the Child.* New York: Farrar, Straus and Giroux.

———. 1991. "The Mistreated Child in the Lamentations of Jeremiah." In *Breaking Down the Wall of Silence: The Liberating Experience of Facing Painful Truth,* 14-26. New York: Dutton.

Miller, P.D. 1984. *The Message of the Psalms: A Theological Commentary.* Minneapolis, Minn.: Augsburg.

Miller, P.D., ed. 1994. *They Cried to the Lord: The Form and Theology of Biblical Prayer.* Minneapolis, Minn.: Fortress.

Mintz, A. 1982. "The Rhetoric of Lamentations and the Representation of Catastrophe." *Prooftexts* 2: 1-17.

Miscall, P.D. 1993. *Isaiah.* Sheffield: JSOT.

Moyers, B. 1999. *Fooling with Words: A Celebration of Poets and Their Craft.* New York: William Morrow.

Newsom, C.A. 1992. "Response to Norman K. Gottwald, 'Social Class and Ideology in Isaiah 40-55.'" *Semeia* 59: 73-78.

Newsom, C.A., and S. Ringe, eds. 1998. *The Women's Bible Commentary: Expanded Edition with Apocrypha.* Rev. ed. Louisville, Ky.: Westminster/John Knox.

Niger, S. 1947. "Yiddish Poets of the 'The Third Destruction.'" *Reconstructionist* (June 27): 13-18.

O'Connor, K.M. 1988. *The Confessions of Jeremiah: Their Interpretation and Role in Chapters 1-25.* Society of Biblical Literature Disserations Series 94. Atlanta, Ga.: Scholars Press.

———. 1998a. "Crossing Borders: Biblical Studies in a Transcultural World." In *Teaching the Bible: The Discourses and Politics of Biblical Pedagogy,* edited by F.F. Segovia and M.A. Tolbert, 322-337. Maryknoll, N.Y.: Orbis Books.

———. 1998b. "Lamentations." In *The Women's Bible Commentary: Expanded Edition with Apocrypha,* rev. ed., edited by C. Newsom and S. Ringe, 187-191. Louisville, Ky.: Westminster/John Knox.

———. 1998c. "The Tears of God and the Divine Character in Jeremiah 2-9." In *God in the Fray: A Tribute to Walter Brueggemann,* edited by T. Linafelt and T.K. Beal, 172-185. Minneapolis, Minn.: Fortress.

———. 1999. "'Speak Tenderly to Jerusalem': Second Isaiah's Reception and Use of Daughter Zion." *Princeton Seminary Bulletin* 3: 281-294.

———. 2001. "Lamentations." *New Interpreters Bible.* Nashville: Abingdon. 6:1011-1072.

Otto, R. 1950. *The Idea of the Holy: An Inquiry into the Non-Rational Factor in the Idea of the Divine and Its Relation to the Rational.* New York: Oxford University Press.

Panikkar, R. 1995. *Invisible Harmony: Essays on Contemplation and Responsibility.* Minneapolis, Minn.: Fortress.

Pham, X.H.T. 1999. *Mourning in the Ancient Near East and the Hebrew Bible.* Journal for the Study of the Old Testament Supplement 302. Sheffield: Sheffield Academic Press.

Pilch, J.J., and B.J. Malina, eds. 1993. *Biblical Social Values and Their Meaning: A Handbook*. Peabody, Mass.: Hendrickson.

Pinault, D. 1992. *The Shiites: Ritual and Popular Piety in a Muslim Community*. New York: St. Martin's Press.

Pleins, D. 1992. *The Psalms: Songs of Tragedy, Hope, and Justice*. Maryknoll, N.Y.: Orbis Books.

Pontifical Biblical Commission. 1994. "The Interpretation of the Bible in the Church," *Origins* 23, no. 29: 498-524.

Provan, I. 1991a. *Lamentations*. New Century Bible Commentary. Grand Rapids, Mich.: Eerdmans.

———. 1991b. "Past, Present, and Future in Lamentations III, 52-66: The Case for Precative Perfect Re-Examined." *Vetus Testamentum* 16, no. 2: 164-175.

Raabe, P.R. 1996. *Obadiah*. Anchor Bible 24D. New York: Doubleday.Re'emi, A.P. 1984. *God's People in Crisis*. International Theological Commentary 19. Grand Rapids, Mich.: Eerdmans.

Renard, J. 1998. *Windows on the House of Islam*. Berkeley and Los Angeles: University of California Press.

Renkema, J. 1998. *Lamentations: Historical Commentary of the Old Testament*. Leuven: Peters.

Reyburn, W.D. 1995. *A Handbook on Lamentations*. New York: United Bible Societies.

Rigby, C. 1997. *Power, Powerlessness, and the Divine: New Inquiries in the Bible and Theology*. Atlanta, Ga.: Scholars Press.

Ronen, R. 1994. *Possible Worlds in Literary Theory*. Cambridge: Cambridge University Press.

Rosenfeld, A.H., and I. Greenberg, eds. 1978. *Confronting the Holocaust: The Impact of Elie Wiesel*. Bloomington, Ind.: Indiana University Press.

Roth, J.K., and M. Berenbaum, eds. 1989. *Holocaust: Religious and Philosophical Implications*. St. Paul, Minn.: Paragon House.

Sachs, N. 1982. "Chorus of Solacers." In *Versions of Survival: The Holocaust and the Human Spirit*, edited by Lawrence L. Langer. Albany, N.Y.: State University of New York Press.

Salters, R.B. 1998. "Searching for Pattern in Lamentations." *Old Testament Essays* 11: 93-104.

Sawyer, J.F.A. 1989. "Daughter of Zion and Servant of the Lord in Isaiah." *Journal for the Study of the Old Testament* 44: 89-107.

Scarry, E. 1985. *The Body in Pain*. New York: Oxford University Press.

Schlosser, E. 1997. "A Grief Like No Other." *The Atlantic Monthly* 280, no. 3 (September): 37-76.

Schor, J.B. 1998. *The Overspent American: Upscaling, Downshifting, and the New Consumer*. New York: Basic Books.

Schreiter, R. 1992. *Reconciliation: Mission and Ministry in a Changing Social Order*. Maryknoll, N.Y.: Orbis Books.

Schwarz, R.M. *The Curse of Cain: The Violent Legacy of Monotheism*. Chicago: University of Chicago Press.

Seidman, N. 1992. "Burning the Book of Lamentations." In *Out of the Garden: Women Writers on the Bible*, edited by D. Buchmann and C. Spiegel. New York: Fawcett Columbine.

Shea, W.H. 1979. "The *qinah* Structure of the Book of Lamentations." *Biblica* 60: 103-107.

Smith-Christopher, D. 1997. "Reassessing the Historical and Sociological Impact of the Babylonian Exile (597/587-539 BCE)." In *Exile: Old Testament, Jewish and Christian Options*, edited by J.M. Scott, 7-36. Journal for the Study of Judaism. London: E.J. Brill.

Soelle, D. 2001. *The Silent Cry: Mysticism and Resistance*. Minneapolis: Fortress.

Soll, J.W. 1992. "Acrostic." *The Anchor Bible Dictionary*. Vol. 1. New York: Doubleday.

Somer, B.D. 1998. *A Prophet Reads Scripture: Allusion in Isaiah 40-66*. Contraversions: Jews and Other Differences. Stanford, Calif.: Stanford University Press.

Song, C.S. 1981. *The Tears of Lady Meng: A Parable of the People's Political Theology*. Risk 11. Geneva: World Council of Churches.

Stulman, L. 1998. *Order Amid Chaos: Jeremiah as Symbolic Tapestry*. The Biblical Seminar 57. Sheffield: Sheffield Academic Press.

Teichman, M., and S. Leder, eds. 1994. *Truth and Lamentation: Stories and Poems of the Holocaust*. Urbana, Ill.: University of Illinois Press.

Townes, E.M., ed. 1993. *A Troubling in My Soul*, Maryknoll, N.Y.: Orbis Books.

Tull-Willey, P. 1997. *Remember the Former Things: The Recollection of Previous Texts in Second Isaiah*. Atlanta, Ga.: Scholars Press.

Wallace, M.I. 1995. *Fragments of the Spirit: Nature, Violence and the Renewal of Creation*. New York: Continuum.

Walton, C. 1996. *When There Are No Words: Finding Your Way to Cope with Loss and Grief*. Ventura, Calif.: Pathfinder.

Waskow, A. 1995. *Seasons of Our Joy: A Modern Guide to the Jewish Holidays*. Boston: Beacon.

Weems, R. *Battered Love: Marriage, Sex, and Violence in the Hebrew Prophets*. Overtures to Biblical Theology. Minneapolis, Minn.: Fortress.

West, C. 1994. *Race Matters*. New York: Vintage Books.

Westermann, C. 1969. *Isaiah 40-66*. Old Testament Library. Philadelphia: Westminster.

———. 1981. *Praise and Lament in the Psalms*. Atlanta, Ga.: John Knox.

———. 1994. *Lamentations: Issues and Interpretation*. Minneapolis, Minn.: Fortress.

Williams, J.G. 1991. *The Bible, Violence, and the Sacred: Liberation from the Myth of Sanctioned Violence*. San Francisco: HarperCollins.

Wink, W. 1984. *Naming the Powers: The Language of Power in the New Testament*. Philadelphia: Fortress.

Winter, S.L. 1996. "An Unsung Lament: The Suffering of Korean Women Taken for Military Sexual Slavery during World War II." Thesis, San Francisco Theological Seminary.

Wolstertorff, N. 1987. *Lament for a Son*. Grand Rapids, Mich.: Eerdmans.

Yates, W. 1998. "Intersections of Art and Religion: Reflections on Works from the Minneapolis Institute of Arts." *Arts: The Arts in Religious and Theological Studies* 10, no. 1.

Young, I. M. *Justice and the Politics of Difference*. Princeton, N.J.: Princeton University Press, 1990.

Zenger, E. 1994. *A God of Vengeance? Understanding the Psalms of Divine Wrath*. Louisville, Ky.: Westminster/John Knox.

Made in the USA
Coppell, TX
13 August 2020